A Giant Thumbs-Up For Hitchhiking With Larry David

I so enjoyed the book, and join those who could not put it down or stop talking about it!!!
Mary Messersmith – California

Oh my God! What a phenomenal book! I was supposed to be studying decided to read a few pages and couldn't stop. How beautifully written - magical, so much love and emotion in every page. I am in awe. My heart is filled! Wow! Now please tell me if you and miracle are still together - what a love story!!!
Eugenia Dean – Bermuda

Brilliant! I was deeply moved. Thank you.
Alan Brewer –William Morris Endeavor

I read the book this past weekend and was moved to laughter (several times, a rarity for these jaded eyes) and impressed. It's diverse and creative, in terms of both form and content: great leaps of fancy, great jumps from present tense to past, and a terrific and smart and deeply thoughtful romp throughout. A real pleasure!
Nicky Weinstock-VP Chernin Entertainment

The book is hilariously funny and moving and something much more: it makes you think about your own interaction with the people around you, friends and strangers, and what wonderful opportunities you might be missing. I tried it one day, it works!
Carson Morton – Author of "Stealing Mona Lisa"

"Hitchhiking" is a layered book and it's also a funny book. Mr. Dolman offers us what he's learned about making all the pesky stuff-of-life things work. How — dare we say it? — to be happy.
Jack Shea – *The Martha's Vineyard Times*

It is relatable, fun and refreshing. The author has a great way with words, and of course your characteristic synchronicities had to be present, lol! I predict the Bestseller list! I actually read it in one sitting, I was so engrossed in it!!
Gary Dunn – Radio Reporter- *Wall Street Journal*

Paul Dolman shares the company of only two other authors who have made me laugh out loud when reading their books - John Updike & John Kennedy Toole. A modern day "Catcher in the Rye."
Andrew Brandt – Colorado

It is a work of art! I hope that one day I can feel the same feeling of surreal enlightenment that your book exudes, and your quote on page 57... "I realize that hanging on to the past is like carrying around sharp pieces of glass in your pocket. Until you get rid of them, they'll cut you every time you attempt to move forward."
...are words to live by!
Ron Davenport – Connecticut

I just finished the book and all I can say is amazing!!!
Jim Shane – Edgartown

I laughed and cried through the insights on life, love, loss and joy. It is inspiring, inviting and impossible not to find a piece of yourself.
...my mind is a little more open and my heart bigger.
Lynn McDonnell – Greenwich, CT

I love the book! It's brilliant!!
Pete Morrell - Boston

I have laughed, I have cried, and I have laughed and cried at the same time while reading your book. I LOVE IT! It is one of the most refreshing reads I have had in a long time.
Dan Maddox - Nashville, TN

I have never before in my life read a book that I just couldn't read fast enough. I found this to be one the most enjoyable reads I have ever had! I just couldn't wait to see what was going to happen next. It is exciting, funny and redemptive. Do yourself a favor and read it right now. You won't be able to put it down.
Mike Bodayle - North Carolina

I loved the book and the sensitive and perceptive writing.
It has given me inspiration to continue to appreciate each day that I wake up (cancer survivor).
LuCille – Boston, MA

I thought it quite humorous that yesterday I was on the ferry to New York and as I turned in my seat, in view were three other people reading the book!!
Mark Badum - New York, NY

"I know where you're coming from. Sometimes you just have to stick out the old thumb"

Larry David 2009

HITCHHIKING
WITH
LARRY DAVID

For all the people throughout my life who have picked me up when I really needed a lift.

Thank You!

HITCHHIKING

WITH

LARRY DAVID

A True Story

From Martha's Vineyard

By

PAUL SAMUEL DOLMAN

© 2010

South Beach Publishing

Nashville, TN

Published by

South Beach Publishing

PO Box 150991

Nashville, TN 37215

Copyright © 2010 by Paul Samuel Dolman

www.hitchhikingwithlarrydavid.com

ISBN: 978-1- 890115-08-1

First Paperback Edition

July 2010

Book Edited by Peter Dergee

Cover Design by Brooke Miracle

"Every branch of human knowledge if traced up to its source and final principles vanishes into mystery."

-Arthur Machen

~I Believe in Miracles~

Intro

In the summer of 1974, Steven Spielberg and I arrived in Martha's Vineyard. I came for a family vacation, he came to shoot the movie "Jaws." Which I assumed, given the title, was about my mother.

Quite simply, it was love at first sight. I stepped off the plane and knew; this is where I belong. There was magic in the wind, and I could immediately taste the sea on my lips, though to this day Dad insists it was the saltwater taffy from the gift shop. Either way this place felt like home.

Both the world and I have changed a lot in the last thirty-five years, yet this magical little Isle has managed to stay relatively unspoiled. Though I have traveled far and wide, the Vineyard has always been my sanctuary. It's the one place I can completely let go and see the extraordinary in the ordinary.

Aside from the occasional 'borrowed' bike or the sight of me strolling along the nude beach, there is no real crime here. The Vineyard is safe enough to leave the front door open, the keys hanging in the ignition, and even do a little hitchhiking.

One sunny day, I stuck out my thumb, and the actor, comedian and Homo Sapien* Larry David pulled over and picked me up. Aside from changing a few names to avoid compromising anyone's privacy, or more importantly being sued, all of the events, no matter how surreal they appear, are entirely true. I even considered changing Larry's name, but given the title...

And now my friend, sit back, relax, and enjoy the ride.

*Attorney's Note: *Homo sapiens*, or humans, are bipedal primates in the family Hominidae and is in no way meant as a connotation of Mr. David's sexual preference.

-1-

We Make Contact

Larry: (Leaning back as I get in the car)

Umm... You're not a serial killer or something, are you?

With its New England charm and captivating beauty, the Vineyard sits nobly off the base of Cape Cod, a mere seven miles from what most of us consider reality. With her pristine beaches and endless miles of green space, the Island feels like heaven. There are no traffic lights, billboards, highways, or malls on this rock. An unguarded feeling permeates people's attitudes and tends to relax their faces. Yes I know, it sounds almost un-American, but this is precisely the charm of the place.

Finding myself at the age of forty-eight in waters without wind, I return to the Vineyard once again. My hope is that the old Island magic will heal some recent wounds and maybe a few past ones too.

Like the Humphrey Bogart character Rick in the film *Casablanca*, I am here because of heartbreak. Though in fairness to Rick, his relationship ended with the reemergence of Victor Laslow. Mine went down from my own mistakes.

A brief history...

Two years ago I met a captivating woman, and we began a glorious run. Unfortunately, I was a bit afraid of commitment (okay, I was completely terrified) and hid behind a wall of excuses designed to keep the exit door open. Despite her loving efforts, I kept pushing her away until she began to look for someone else.

We broke up, and if that wasn't painful enough, we continued to spend time together even after she began seeing other people. I would not commit and could not let go. Finally this self-created limbo hell got to be too much, and I fled. My inner homing device kicked in, and I decided to return to the Vineyard.

For this to happen, I faced a few practical challenges.

After a self-imposed six-year sabbatical from mainstream life, I could not afford to lease a place. Summer rental rates are just too high for the average, unemployed plebeian. If I wanted to be on the Island, I had no choice but to stay with…

(Cue Jaws theme)… my parents!

An Overview of the Parental Underbelly…

Every summer my parents migrate by wagon train from Saint Augustine, Florida to a tiny cabin in Martha's Vineyard. When visiting them, you never know what to expect. It could be peaceful (three days max) or a harrowing hellhole (anything longer than a week and you have only yourself to blame). You may be welcome (Mom) or you may not (Dad). Through the years their roles have become well defined; Mom invites you to stay as long as you like, Dad makes you feel unwelcome as soon as you arrive.

It's not all Dad's fault. He only has the social energy to be nice to humans for about ten minutes a day. This allotment of pleasantries is usually exhausted at the supermarket or on the phone with a customer service representative.

The truth has always been illusive in our family, with the level of veracity hovering just below *Pravda*. For example, despite claims to the contrary, Mom and Dad spend most of their time in front of the television. They prefer old films, reruns, and news programs warning them of impending doom. Though I never remember to do it, when dealing with them, here is what works best: don't ever ask them to step outside their comfort zone.

The Five Deadly Questions

Does anyone want to…

Visit Edgartown?

Watch the sunset?

Go somewhere?

Anywhere?

Change the routine in any conceivable way?

The routine is so locked in, Mom has even written out the summer breakfast schedule and posted it on the refrigerator…Monday-eggs…Tuesday-bagel…Wednesday… It is <u>NEVER</u> altered. (As a practical joke I considered rearranging and reprinting the schedule. But I was afraid with such a dramatic shift one of them might get sick.)

I cope with their eccentricities by spending most of my time away from the *Parental Asylum*. On a typical day, I bicycle for hours, swim in the chilly waters of the Atlantic, and hitchhike around the Island. Yes, I could get around the Island on my bike, public transportation, or with my parents car, but I would miss out on countless fascinating encounters. That is why I stick out my thumb.

After years of hitching on this Island, I have become familiar with the tenets of its unwritten code, which I share with you now…

The Official MVY Hitchhiker's Manifesto™

Stand up straight and keep your hands out of your pockets. No shades or hats, and you better not have a backpack (it could have a bomb in it). Smile a lot. Sincerely if possible, insincerely if hung over. Clean is always better than filthy.

It's easier for one person to get a ride than two, unless you're with a woman. An obvious rule of thumb; the prettier the girl, the faster the ride (just like in life). A gorgeous woman alone will get a ride immediately, and if she's seriously hot, may cause a major pile-up. Trying to hitch with three people is extremely difficult, and a group of guys wearing turbans, next to impossible.

It's much harder to hitch with a dog, unless it's a puppy or a yellow lab. Stay away from farm livestock, or God forbid, any creature that appears to be rabid or what is traditionally considered a wild animal (i.e., lions, bears, cobras, etc.).

Your best times of operation are during the daylight hours. It's very challenging at night, at least until the bars get out. But then you run the risk of getting into a car with a drunken maniac. Being maimed or crippled in a bad accident would probably put a damper on your summer.

After being picked up, politely attempt some kind of conversation with the occupants, and based on the response, take your cue from there. Any mumbling, hitting, or biting by the driver is a sign to keep quiet for the remainder of the trip.

The older the driver, the less likely the ride. "Those lazy kids should walk like we used to. The world is going to hell, I tell you." Yet ironically, older cars stop more frequently than newer ones, especially old Volvos. (Save the whales!) Convertibles, classic cars, and Jeeps with no tops tend to stop a lot. Yuppies in SUVs, repairmen, commercial vans, motorcycles, police vehicles, tour buses, ice cream trucks, and tractors almost never do.

Lastly, it is bad form to flip people off if they pass you by. This rule applies no matter how long you have been standing in the rain while being eaten alive by mosquitoes. Like in life, it's best not to take the rejection personally.

~~~

With the sun on my face, I stand by the road for the first official hitch of the season. Within a moment a shiny blue Volvo convertible appears on the horizon. The driver is an older, white-haired lion I immediately recognize as the famous author and historian David McCullough *(John Adams and Truman)*. My lucky day! This is why I enjoy hitchhiking.

As a huge admirer of Mr. McCullough's work, I make an executive decision, wherever he's going, I'm going that way.

This is a once-in-a-lifetime opportunity to ask a great fountainhead of wisdom all kinds of deep questions. I am sure to learn a few transcendent truths. In fact, I bet he and I have so much in common we'll become fast friends... Island comrades... a Dynamic Duo... maybe we can even team up to ..."

HE IS SLOWING DOWN! OKAY, HERE WE GO...

"I would give you a lift. (Yes!) But I'm only going a couple thousand feet up the road. (What?) Sorry." (NO!)

Our blockbuster buddy movie comes to a screeching halt and careens straight off the road into a ditch. Devastated, I fall away from the sun like Icarus.

After a brief period of sitting Shiva by the side of the road, I bounce back with the mantra, "Not to worry, the perfect car will pick me up." Maybe the lessons of *The Secret* really work, though I've been a bit skeptical ever since *The Prosperity Center* went out of business. I decide to give it a try and begin to visualize...a vintage car filled with Swedish nannies...headed to the beach for a little fun and they have packed a gourmet lunch they wish to share.

Let's see how this works out.

The next car approaches (okay, here we go)... My thumb goes out... No sign of blond hair (no problem, I'm not picky)... It looks like an older guy (maybe he's just the driver)... He's slowing down (sinking a bit)... No nannies (going down)... The guy is balding with glasses (completely deflated)...

Cut to…

(Car pulls over)

Larry David: Need a ride?

Hitchhiker: Yes. Thank you.

Larry: (Leaning back as I get in)

Umm… You're not a serial killer or something, are you?

Hitchhiker:

Even if I am, it's the Vineyard, and I'm on vacation. I'm not working.

Larry: (laughs, shakes my hand, and we drive off)

2

The Gospel of Seinfeld

Larry: You know I never pick up hitchhikers.

Hitchhiker: Really?

Larry: Really.

Hitchhiker: Not a bad commandment to live by.

(Pauses)

But why me?

Larry: I have no idea. I just felt like I was supposed to.

Larry David created the television show *Seinfeld*. You might have heard of it. The show was a highly commercial, critical favorite that *TV Guide* named the greatest television program of all time. *Seinfeld* was on the air for nine years and is considered by many to be a cultural phenomenon. Yet all of this was somehow accomplished without me viewing a single episode. Go figure. My parents make up for my *Seinfeld* viewing delinquency by watching the reruns religiously. (There is a scientific explanation for all this: researchers believe the television-watching gene tends to skip a generation.)

Tonight is no exception, as I return home to find them in *Seinfeld* heaven. "Mom, Dad, you won't believe who picked me up hitchhiking… Larry David!"

"Really? We love his stuff." Mom points towards the glowing box and says, "Have you seen this episode?"

"No. I, um, I never watch any television." (The clock stops ticking.)

They both look at me like I just told them I was a cannibal. "What? Never?"

Not to worry; I can bridge this gap. "Well now, which one of these characters is Jerry?"

"Jerry is Jerry." Mom says.

"Okay. So Jason Alexander is Jason?"

"No." Dad chimes in, "Jason is George." My parents burst into hysterics.

"How come you and the laugh track howl when the guy with the strange haircut walks in?"

"Because Kramer is funny."

"But he didn't say anything yet."

"Kramer is funny."

"But he didn't say anything humorous, he just walked in."

Dad ignores my observations. "It's about life and other stuff…"

"And Kramer is funny."

"Yes." The soundtrack roars and they laugh again. "You should sit down and watch this."

"No thanks. Hey, I've got an idea. How about the three of us go down to the beach and watch the sunset? Maybe we could bring a blanket and a bottle of wine."

"Are you crazy?" Dad says in shock. "And miss *Seinfeld*?"

"But you watch these reruns every night."

"I've seen enough sunsets. Seen one, seen them all." And with that, he turns it up and tunes me out.

Defeated in my quixotic campaign of parental enlightenment, I retreat to the bedroom and pick up one of my favorite books, *The Prophet*. In Gibran's masterpiece, every phrase feels divinely inspired. I randomly open it and read, "The depth and connection of love is never truly known until the moment it is lost."

My phone rings. It's the girl, the one I call The Miracle.

~~~~~

Flashback:

It's the day after Christmas in sunny Del Mar. A friend arrives from Los Angeles with the well-known spiritual author, Dick Sutphen, writer of the bestselling book 'Soul Agreements.' The three of us share the day and discuss, among other things, the mysterious topic of soul mates.

12

Dick's Wellspring of Wisdom

Do they really exist?   *Yes, most certainly.*

Do we have only one in a lifetime?   *Not necessarily.*

How do we find them?   *Follow your heart.*

How will we know when we meet them? Trust me, you will know.

Does love between souls transcend death?   Absolutely.

I share what has been happening with me recently, and Dick says, "It sounds as though you may soon meet your soul mate."

"Well, it is going to take a miracle for that to happen." I say sarcastically.

The next day I get a call from a woman I met on Myspace inviting me for tea. An hour later I walk down the block and meet her at a seaside cafe. She suddenly insists, "You have to meet my roommate. I feel like you two would really connect."

"Sure, maybe later this week."

"I'm picking her up from the airport tonight, and she's leaving for Aspen in the morning. So it has to be this evening. How about I call my boyfriend, and the four of us have dinner?"

I agree, and Miss Myspace drives off.

A few hours later, the three of them walk through my door. Her roommate is stunningly beautiful: olive skin, green eyes, flowing sun-streaked hair, and a smile that could melt a wall of ice. Yet she lacks the pretense usually accompanying such a stunning storefront.

I love the sound of her voice; the resonant tones, the calming phrases, and the careful consideration of her words. We finish each other's sentences and share a common worldview. This woman totally gets me, sees me, and feels me.

As we are preparing the meal our eyes lock, allowing me to see an even greater beauty within. There is a depth, a compassion, a softness, a sensitivity unlike anything I have experienced. An unexplainable familiarity exists between us that we openly acknowledge. Crossing paths in the kitchen, we spontaneously embrace. I can't help myself and say, "Holding you feels like coming home."

She blushes.

Who is this person? How do I know her? What is happening here?

We enjoy a delicious dinner of Pasta Pauley-Vera then settle into a long, interesting conversation. Near midnight I say to the beautiful roommate, "This is great, but don't you need to go home and sleep? Otherwise, you'll be exhausted for your ski trip."

"Oh, I decided not to go. On the flight back home I was reading this fascinating book by Dick Sutphen called 'Soul Agreements,' and it changed my perspective on dating.

I've decided not to waste any more time and wait for the real thing."

"What?" I literally fall off the couch. I mean, of all the books in the world to mention? "I spent yesterday with Dick Sutphen in this room discussing soul mates!"

She then falls off the couch on top of me.

The next day we are signing in for a yoga class when I see her surname happens to be... MIRACLE!

"Miracle? Miracle is your last name?"

She smiles.

"Really?" I say, incredulous.

"Since the day I was born."

After our class we go for a long walk on the beach, and for the first time, I gently take her hand in mine. The day turns into night, and before long, fourteen hours has flown by.

Before she leaves I ask, "Can I show you a recent entry in my journal?" She nods yes. "Here, look at this. 'It's going to take a <u>miracle</u> for me to find someone to share my soul with.' I had no idea my words would be taken so literally."

She laughs and adds, "There are so many signs."

As she pulls out of the driveway, I realize I already miss her. Something beautiful is happening.

The next day, a highly intuitive friend pulls me aside and says of the Miracle, "I'm not saying she is the one, but she's the one."

Instead of leaving after ten days as planned, I stay in Del Mar for the next three months. The two of us spend every minute together, and when it's time for me to return to Nashville, the Miracle comes home with me.

Over the next two years we spend our days rediscovering each other for the first time.

~~~~~

It's been weeks since the Miracle and I have spoken, and I'm still feeling guarded. Should I pick it up? I decide to take the chance.

"Well, I'm surprised you called."

"Should I leave you alone?"

There is a long silence on my part. "How's it going?"

"How are you doing?"

"Tell me about you. Anything new?"

"How's the Island?"

"It's the Vineyard."

We share a couple more moments of awkward silence, a few superficial responses, and hang up. Funny, part of me really wanted to connect, but as soon as I heard her voice I shut down.

Even though my choices helped create our collapse, I am still feeling angry and hurt, so our separation is for the best. If there is any hope for me to heal, I will need more time and space.

My heart aches for her and for us. Between my parents and the breakup, I feel like an unwelcome, broken-hearted exile on the Island of Elba.

"The depth and connection of love is never truly known until the moment it is lost."

Now I know, but it feels too late.

3

Jewish Boating

Larry: By the way, are you Jewish?

Hitchhiker: Are you?

Larry: (Shoots me a look that says, 'Are you kidding?')

Hitchhiker: I think my actual lineage is mongrel.

Larry: (Thinking for a moment)

That's good enough for me.

Thirty-five years ago my parents bought some land in the woods of outer Edgartown. For years they scrimped, saved, clipped coupons, cut corners and fought like mad to build a place. Though I should point out, all the combat was done exclusively with each other. Mom was the driving force behind building it while Dad was *unofficially* against the project. He waged a campaign of passive resistance that Gandhi himself would have envied. But to be fair to Dad, his default setting is NO. He's pretty much against any initiative that requires him to leave his seat.

The *Parental Asylum* sits nestled at the dead end of a dirt road, so there's never much traffic. With its cedar walls, the place is rustic and down home. Mom's choice of decorating motif? Early American Cluttered. The counters and walls are covered in a variety of garage sale nick-knacks (i.e., General Robert. E. Lee Memorial Tea Set, a tattered map of Armenia, a list of Reader's Digest Top-Ten Jigsaw Puzzles, old pictures of Clark Gable).

I point towards what looks like an old ice pick. "Hey Mom, what's this?"

"Oh be careful with that. I bought that a couple years ago at the Bishop's garage sale. It's a Pope Pius XII pick ax."

All of this junk is thrown together in the same way birds tend to grab anything when building a nest. Mom's designing mantra is 'let no space go unused.' If there is any rhyme or reason to all this decorative chaos, you'll have to get Stephen Hawking to help you figure it out.

Their Miniature Daschund is the last member of our strange aggregation. Max has the honor of being the only carbon-based life form my parents feel comfortable having around. Every day he barks at anything that moves. Last week, in an effort to shake life up around the house, Max added things that don't move to his repartee. This is Mom's cue to say in a stern voice, "No barking." Five minutes later, he's back at it again, followed by the familiar refrain, "No barking."

Since this pattern of futility has gone on consistently for ten years, I'm going to go out on a limb here and say, Max doesn't seem to get it. Another one of Max's annual rituals is getting skunked. I guess he hasn't figured that one out either.

For some reason, every time I reach for Max, one of my parents will say, "Don't hurt him." Having never harmed an animal in my life, I can't figure out why my actions require these repeated warnings. After some reflection, I conclude this phrase must be some kind of unique blessing bestowed upon the breed. So, in an effort to fit in, every time one of them touches Max, I also say, "Don't hurt him."

Feeling a bit sad from last night's aborted Miracle call, I leave the confines of the *Parental Asylum* and ride my bike about ten miles to Alley's. This funky little general store was founded about 150 years ago, which also happens to be the last time it was cleaned. Okay, I'm slightly exaggerating; it's actually charming. Alley's is a convenient stop for any wayfarer headed up Island and a fertile spot to hitchhike. There is a real voodoo to the place. No matter how random my request may be, every time I walk in, I find exactly what I desire. "Do you happen to have organic, blueberry, raccoon's milk non-fat ice cream with raisins?"

"Yes, it's right across from the nuclear fusion set."

Today I keep it simple with a cup of coffee. I walk out and across the parking lot, lean my bike on a tree, and stick out my thumb to the infinite possibilities of the moment.

My first ride looks like it drove straight out of *The Great Gatsby*: a candy red, vintage Mercedes convertible with tan leather seats. Mike is a handsome former financial guy from New York. Abiding by *The Official MVY Hitchhiking Manifesto*^{TM}, I get in and ask, "Are you on vacation?"

"No, I unintentionally ended up with the whole summer off." I look at him curiously, and he continues, "I was recently downsized."

"I'm sorry."

"Don't be. It was difficult at first, but probably for the best. I was burned out on the whole Wall Street charade and ready for a change. The job was sucking the life out of me. The merger just hurried me out the door."

"So, now what?"

"To tell you the truth, I have no idea. My being here all season is part of the process of discovering what's next."

"Any luck?"

He laughs, "None. I have no earthly idea what the future holds for me."

I reach out and extend my hand, "Join the club." We shake and I add, "I guess we've become high-end Vineyard vagrants."

"That's a nice way to look at it. How long are you here?"

"A couple of weeks. Unless my dad runs me off early."

"Back at home are you?"

I nod. "And you thought being fired was depressing."

"What about staying at the campground?"

"I would, but I look bad in one of those wife-beater tee shirts."

Though we are technically strangers, our conversation becomes surprisingly intimate. Wall Street Mike is very open and honest about his feelings, finances, and fears. "This recent economic meltdown has me questioning my old values. For years I worked my ass off and made a lot of money. But in the end, it left me empty. At this stage in my life, I feel like I'm reevaluating everything."

I realize there's something here allowing him to open up. It's almost as if he has been waiting a long time to share his inner treasures, if only someone was kind enough to ask. Maybe, we are all like that?

"Speaking of money, here is the million dollar question: How do you sleep at night?"

Wall Street Mike smiles, "Deeply. Well, ever since I got to the Island."

"The Vineyard does that to people."

I know *Society's Rules That Don't Work* clearly state: We should all mind our own business and keep the topics on a highly superficial level. "Howareyou? Fineandyou? Fineandyou? Fineandyou? Fineandyou?" Preferably said by not missing a beat, taking a breath, or most importantly, making any kind of authentic connection.

But maybe with courage and the genuine desire to connect, we can break through the inauthentic ice. I don't mind being this guy; in fact I like it. This is why I love to hitchhike.

Each encounter carries the potential for spiritual riches. Or as Mark Twain so eloquently said, "Nothing so liberalizes a man and expands the kindly instincts that nature put in him as travel and contact with many kinds of people."

It's as if the universe is a hologram, and its infinite truth lies deep within each of us. These jewels may be uncovered by the right question, or more importantly, by allowing enough space between the answers. We only need to be open to access this abundance.

Wall Street Mike drops me off at the Chilmark Store, and I'm immediately reminded why I love this place: the old-time porch with its rocking chairs, people from all walks of life immersed in conversation, kids running around with popsicles, and the smell of the Island's best pizza wafting through the salty sea air.

I grab my first slice of the season and take a front row seat with an unobstructed view of the festivities. Soon I'm chatting with one of the local celebrities, Harold Ramis. He has had enormous success in the film business: acting (*Ghostbusters*), directing (*Groundhog Day, Caddyshack and Analyze This*), and writing (*Animal House*). Harold is a great storyteller and today is no exception as he describes the follies surrounding the promotion of his latest film.

The attorney Alan Dershowitz arrives. Alan is a controversial figure who has defended many high-profile clients like O.J Simpson and Claus Von Bulow. The film "*Reversal of Fortune*" was based on Alan's book about the Von Bulow case. But today Alan is just another guy in an old shirt on his way to the beach.

In the midst of this enjoyable chaos, a woman around my age asks, "Do you mind if I sit here?" I nod and she plops down next to me with her own slice. "I'm Nancy." We shake hands and start raving about the pizza.

"Where are you from?" I ask.

"Beverly Hills, though I hate to tell people. I'm not sure I fit in there." I can see why. She carries none of the pretension (or botox) usually associated with that zip code. To me she feels more natural and organic, like someone from Vermont who raises autistic goats on a biodegradable farm.

"Why do you feel like you don't fit in out there?"

"There are a lot of reasons. The pace, it's so materialistic, and I hate all the traffic." She pauses and looks around, "I really like it here."

"Me too."

She thinks for a minute. "I guess the hardest part of being there has been watching my teenage boy struggle. He's a great kid, but we have had a lot of ups and downs with him. Los Angeles is a tough place to be a teenager."

"I find it a tough place to be a biped."

"You're right." She smiles. "It's been a stressful couple of years, but hopefully we've turned a corner. I'm sorry, I didn't mean to dump all this on you."

"Please don't apologize for being authentic. I'm flattered. I can't imagine what it feels like to raise a child and then surrender that precious being to society. I have never had the courage to make that choice."

"Maybe someday you will."

"Maybe."

"Are you married?"

"No and my relationship of a couple of years just went up in flames. Maybe I should find a bride through the internet?"

"You don't want to go that far."

"I've decided to give it six more months and if I still haven't met anyone, I'm going to Lourdes."

After a while her husband joins us, shaking my hand while scanning the porch for someone more notable to approach. After a moment, he steps away to schmooze a more important life form.

Nancy shares a secret. "He would not want me to tell you this, but he is a very successful power broker in Hollywood."

Watching him flutter around the porch, he could also pass for some kind of highly-caffeinated prehistoric bird. A species once hunted into extinction by much deadlier predators who evolved into the people who run large corporations.

The Hollywood Birdman returns, and after about an hour of pleasant give and take, he surprises me with, "Would you like to join us for a little Jewish Boating?"

"For a little what?"

"Jewish boating. Come on, we'll have fun."

Having never experienced Jewish boating, I am intrigued and say yes.

We drive down to the dock and climb into his high-tech motorboat. Taking a spin around the gorgeous confines of Menemsha Pond, we pass by James Taylor's spectacular home. It's a picture-perfect day and the scenery is stunning. Ever since I was a kid, I have loved being on the water.

The captain inquires, "Well, what do you think?"

"It's wonderful and reminds me of my first days in a boat a long time ago…"

~~~~~

Flashback:

It is a cloudless Sunday morning. In our small rented rowboat, we leave civilization and venture deep into the backwaters of the Florida Everglades in search of fish. With his ever-present two-dollar transistor radio in hand, Dad soaks up the scenery. I listen to the tinny sound of the Carpenter's masterpiece, "Top of the World," perfectly capturing the moment in song. This is a far cry from the Brooklyn tenement housing my father grew up in.

My friend Jeff and I dutifully do the oar work. It's demanding, but inspired by the beauty of our surroundings, the ten-year-old crew is not complaining. The alligators eye us warily from the shore. Wait a minute. On second thought it's us who are leery of them.

We come out here a lot and often allow the current to take us where it wishes. We watch cranes stalk fish and otters play with the abandon of children. Though we rarely ever catch anything, nothing takes away from our time of reverence in this aquatic cathedral.

Dad and I find peace here.

~~~~

The Hollywood Birdman looks at me, raises his arms and says, "Jewish boating!"

Since we never perform any religious rituals during the expedition, I fail to discover the difference between Jewish, or say, Hindu boating.

As we pull into the dock and grab our stuff, I deliver the famous *Godfather* line, "Leave the gun, take the cannoli." Nancy points to her husband and says, "That's the one he always uses!" This must be a secret bonding code because The Hollywood Birdman surprises me again with, "Would you like to come back and see our place?"

I go with the flow, and soon we're making our way down a long and winding driveway. We come upon a low-key estate overlooking one of the prettiest beaches I have ever seen. The views are breathtaking. While we are relaxing at the house, Nancy says, "Remember, you have a golf date tomorrow with Larry."

Sensing something I ask, "Larry David?"

"Yes." The Hollywood Birdman says. "How did you know?"

"He picked me up hitchhiking."

"No he didn't."

"I'm serious, he did. Three days ago."

He insists, "But Larry NEVER picks up hitchhikers!"

"This time he did. I swear."

The Hollywood Birdman ponders this, then texts Larry the cryptic message, "I'm sitting in my bedroom with Nancy and the Hitchhiker…"

As the sun begins its final descent, I realize I need to get on my bike and ride back to Edgartown. Nancy gives me a lift back to Alleys, and a few minutes later I am peddling towards home. About halfway there I come to a fork in the road. I can go home for dinner or head into Edgartown to return a few phone calls. Though hungry, I choose the latter. I have no idea at the time, but this simple decision will have a profound impact on my summer.

4

The Larry Phenomenon

Hitchhiker: Do you believe in magic?

Larry: (Shrugs) Nahhhh...

(Phe·nom·e·non- Pronunciation: \fi-ˈnä-mə-ˌnän, : an exceptional, unusual, or abnormal person, thing, or occurrence)*

I arrive in Edgartown during the *Magic Hour*, that last hour of the day when the light is soft and the hues are warm. This village looks like something Walt Disney would have created and called *New England Town*. Coming down Main Street feels like riding into a postcard: picture-perfect houses painted annually in white, immaculate gardens with long picket fences, the police directing traffic on narrow one-way streets, small shops lining the lanes, and sitting stoically at the top of Main in all her colonial splendor, the old Whaling Church.

Turning left down Water Street, I pass old captains' houses with their widow walks and roses in full bloom. I can smell the honeysuckle blossoms as I ride by quaint cottages with welcoming front porches. The sun floods the harbor with a palette of pastels and streaking light, bestowing ethereal blessings upon me. I stop at the Edgartown Wharf to return my calls but fail to get a signal.

On the move again, I run into Mr. Flakey. Every year we share a circular exercise in futility I have christened...

Mr. Flakey's Charade

Stage One: We bump into each other, talk for a while, and he tells me to call him to setup a time for us to have lunch.

My interpretation: Call me for lunch = Call me for lunch.

Actual meaning: Call me for lunch = Don't really call, but it's good to see you.

Stage Two: I call, leave a message, he never calls back.

Stage Three: We run into each other again, he says he never got the message, claims to have lost my number, really wants to get together, asks me to call him again to set a time for us to definitely have lunch.

My interpretation: Really wants to get together = Really wants to get together.

Actual meaning: Really wants to get together = Damn, not him again.

Stage Four: We engage in more awkward encounters, he sees me coming and avoids me, I see him coming and avoid him.

Stage Five: Return to Island and begin Stage One…

This summer we are right on schedule when, after a few minutes of small talk, Mr. Flakey begins Stage One.

Silently I wonder, maybe *this* year things will be different. Maybe this summer we will actually break through and break bread. Maybe Mr. Flakey really means it this time. Maybe at last we will transcend *Mr. Flakey's Charade*.

Nahhhhhh!

I say goodbye to Mr. Flakey, find a bench overlooking the harbor, and begin my calls. I'm dialing the phone when someone approaches from the left.

"Excuse me, do you happen to know where the Atlantic…(He gasps!) "Oh my God! What the… Holy Sh—t!"

I'm stunned. "Oh my God! What the… Holy…LARRY?"

Larry is shocked too. "What is going on? Are you a ghost or something?"

I'm speechless for a moment. Then say, "No I'm not a ghost!"

Larry trying to make sense of this asks, "Then how did…"

"Did you get the text about me being in their bedroom?"

"Yes, a few minutes ago. It freaked me out. This is crazy! Wait a minute. Are you on your bike?"

"Yes."

"So you rode twenty-miles. What the hell is going on? How did you get down here so fast?"

"I... This is freaky. I mean the same day? It's a phenomenon!"

Then almost in a prosecuting tone…"Wait a minute…Larry, what are YOU doing down here? You live twenty miles away on the other end of the Island."

Somewhat defensive…"I'm meeting my daughter at the Atlantic for dinner."

Cautiously nodding I say, "Okay…"

"I got lost. Speaking of which, do you happen to know where it is?"

"Yes. (Gesturing) It's over there. "It's a good choice, the food's terrific. Larry, what are the odds of this happening?"

"Close to impossible. It's pretty freaky. Okay, I am late and I have to go to dinner."

"Enjoy your evening. I'll see you tomorrow."

"Very funny." Larry laughs and walks off still shaking his head.

For a moment I sit there stunned by the synchronicity.

I text The Hollywood Birdman and tell him what has just happened. His response is succinct. "You are in a very strong place of attraction right now. Be extremely conscious of what you choose to create."

This reminds me of when Obi-Wan Kenobi said, "Use the force, Luke."

I begin to consider the timing required to pull this off, but it all feels beyond me. So many events had to be in precise sequence for this encounter to unfold.

What if I hadn't met The Hollywood Birdman and Nancy? What if I didn't go Jewish Boating, but instead went to the beach as planned? What if I had gone home instead of into town? What if had I chosen to sit somewhere else?

What about the hundreds of circumstances/choices on Larry's side of the table? What happened in his day leading up to the moment we connected?

What if…what if… what if?

Change a moment here or a moment there, and every single thing is different. It's funny, how our whole lives shift with the simplest of choices. This reminds me to stay present and choose from a place of love. I know this is easier said than done, but at the very least, to set the life-bar higher with clear intentions.

Are these chance encounters or Divine Appointments? Meetings set up by a Higher Authority we agree to without our temporal mind's conscious consent? It appears we have no idea what's happening. Yet on a deeper level, semi-unwittingly, we go along for the ride. More often than not, I have found these encounters beneficial, even life-changing. Can such interlocking synchronicity occur totally by chance? While I have no tangible explanation for this, I feel in my bones it is not a coincidence. It feels too organized.

Most importantly who or what orchestrates this process? All of it leaves me wondering…'Is there a vast Intelligence behind the curtain, and when we truly let go do we allow this Intelligence to move through us?'

In the words of Albert Einstein: "Everything is determined…by forces of which we have no control. It is determined for the insect as well as the star. Human beings, vegetables, or cosmic dust—we all dance to a mysterious tune, intoned in the distance by an invisible piper."

Leaving the inner confines of my mind, I look across the water. The harbor appears even more dazzling as a vast panoply of boats find their way back from the frolicking sea. A sleek sailboat with the name *"Believe"* pulls directly in front of me, and I spontaneously cry out, "My God!"

For a few minutes I am silent.

How could I NOT believe?

Yet we all manage to fall into a deep sleep of forgetting, and I am no exception. We suffer from a collective spiritual dementia, where we constantly lose awareness of the ocean of magic in which we exist. And to think we do this while hurtling through space on a giant magnet.

Believe.

In my headphones the Beatles begin singing "All You Need Is Love." The sunset has now reached indescribable proportions. Alas, just another miracle in an infinite and eternal sea of miracles. I sit there ablaze in the glory, grateful that the tiny dot of me plays a small part in the vast opera of Being.

Believe? Indeed!

-5-

No Small Acts

Hitchhiker: I really appreciate the ride.

Larry: Don't mention it.

I wake up to my mother's beaming smile and warm embrace. The early morning is our special time together before Dad wakes up and they merge into a single entity dedicated to solving crossword puzzles. Once a fierce emotional bulldozer full of hectoring advice, Mom has mellowed and become more childlike.

"Good morning my son," she says. We hug and kiss. "Would you like an omelet?"

"Sure. By the way thanks for washing and folding my laundry yesterday. You didn't have to do that."

"You're welcome. I love having you here." She picks up a small notepad and pen. "There is so much to do, I should make a list. Can I make you an omelet for breakfast?"

"Yes, that sounds great."

Over the last year she has begun shedding her short-term memory. Yet in a stroke of universal brilliance, the more she forgets the greater she loves. "Are you hungry? How about an omelet?"

"Yes, I'm starved."

Max comes up and nudges my mother's leg. She bends down to pet him and says, "Oh look, he's letting me know he wants his breakfast."

"Mom, I think you already fed him." Suspecting I may be on to his little food con, Max gives me a guilty glance. At some point Max must have figured out Mom is like a broken ATM, capable of yielding an unending stream of chow and has decided to milk this for all it's worth.

Mom bends down with his second breakfast. "Here's your food, little feller." Max waddles over to his grub, looks up at me as if to say, "Please don't rat me out," and digs in. Since we are both inmates in the same asylum, I choose to remain silent. (Honor amongst thieves.)

While many people become bitter with age (i.e., Dad), Mom is being transformed from a disenchanted cynic into someone who is just happy to be here. So in the polarity of my parents' universe, Mom is the positive Yin to Dad's cranky Yang.

As Mom's social self crumbles away, something infinitely more luminous is emerging. This radiance is what I see when I gaze into her eyes. "Mom, you look great."

"Really?" She glances at herself in the mirror and strokes her hair. "Well, I'm a few inches shorter than my modeling days back in New York." She looks in the mirror again. "But I guess I'm not bad for seventy-nine."

"You look terrific."

She chuckles to herself. "Would you like some breakfast?"

Mom is warm and loving, but you still need to be careful where you step.

Maternal Land Mines to Avoid at Any Cost

*The United States of America (Still the greatest   country in the world!)

*The Democrats (FDR was a heroic and noble man.)

*The mold growing in her house (What the hell can I do about it?)

*Non-organic food (I've lived 80 years eating this poison.)

*Dad (Don't criticize your father!)

*Anything and everything she does.

My age precludes me from enlightening her. The facts be damned, she knows what she knows, and she is always right. This is based solely on Einstein's obscure theory, Longevity = Knowledge[6]. I'm curious about this phenomenon of Mom gaining knowledge through linear time osmosis, as opposed to more traditional methods such as research or personal experience. When asked about this, she offers no insights. Instead, she dismisses my inquiries with a wave of the hand and a shake of the head. "I am not going to get into it."

The television is blaring around the clock with coverage of Michael Jackson's death. (This is the top story on the planet?) Catching a few minutes of his funeral on the tube, held at the sold out Staples Center, I'm struck by how the service resembles a musical variety show with a twist: there is a large gold casket on stage. In between performances from people who have never met the king of pop and maudlin tributes by celebrities, the advertisers try to sell me stuff I don't really need. Ah, America.

Deciding to abandon Michael and my maternal research project, I get on the bike for the easy two-mile ride down to the Among The Flowers Café.

After experiencing *The Larry Phenomenon*, I began my day on the bike with a new mantra: "I surrender to the divine flow. Show me miracles beyond my wildest imagination. Let this be my greatest day."

One of the things I love about the Vineyard is its ability to equalize people socially. Here, the known and the unknown mingle freely. You may be a billionaire or even a movie star, but you still have to wait in line for your cappuccino at Among The Flowers. The inside of the café is about the size of large walk-in closet. The cafe boasts a covered porch and a small garden where dogs and vagrants like myself are welcome. The shop is run with unequalled efficiency by a swarm of girls who manage to keep everyone happy and highly caffeinated.

Today finds me on the porch with fellow Flowers regular, Billionaire Bob. He and I cover the sports scene and catch up on Island news. Though extremely wealthy, he is one of the least pretentious men I have ever met. He is also one of the smartest, and with his thick glasses and mad scientist hairdo, really looks the part.

I've noticed many wealthy people can suffer from an affliction I call *The Billionaire Lean-Back*. Here's how it works. When approached repeatedly by family, friends, or strangers looking for a piece of their gigantic nest egg, the billionaire begins to instinctively lean back. After a while, everyone becomes just another awkward fund request. So, unless they are also wealthy or have a long history of being in the billionaire's proximity without seeking a handout, they are treated with financial trepidation.

Ironically, most of us long to be rich, powerful, and famous, yet these are the very things that isolate us from others. More importantly, these false idols separate us from a true sense of self. In our obsessive desire for more, we end up feeling less.

Later, I'm sitting with a friend when the actress Meg Ryan (*When Harry Met Sally, Sleepless in Seattle*) sits down at the table next to us. As so often happens on this porch, conversations overlap and folks get intertwined in each other's business. Today is no exception, and soon we are chatting with Meg. I like her for a variety of reasons. She is always friendly, walks around with no makeup, and wears nappy old clothes like the rest of us summer mortals. In a way, Meg is the anti-movie movie star.

As we talk, it occurs to me that Meg has had a profound impact on the world's burgeoning consciousness movement. Years ago she gave Oprah Winfrey a book entitled *The Power of Now*, by the spiritual teacher Eckhart Tolle. For a few years, the book collected dust on the mighty Oprah's bookshelf until she picked it up and was deeply moved. By then Tolle had released another book, *A New Earth*, which sold six million copies.

After reading it, Oprah was so inspired she decided to make it the first non-fiction book ever featured by her book club. She also created a worldwide, live web event featuring her and Tolle. The webcast enabled over thirty-five million people around the world to participate and connect.

As I travel down the Meg-Oprah-Eckhart rabbit hole, I am overwhelmed by the scope of its reach. How many lives were touched because one woman gave another woman a book. How simple, yet profound. I realize there are no small acts.

When I share these thoughts with Meg, she says. "Wow, I had no idea the webcasts were such a success and impacted so many people. I'm shocked."

"Tolle himself says you are here to enable the divine purpose of the universe to unfold. That is how important you are." I go on. "One day, back in 1955 in Montgomery Alabama, a woman decided she would not give up her seat on a bus. That choice ignited the Civil Rights Movement. What Rosa Parks did is no different than you handing Oprah that book. This proves, once again, there are no small acts. "

Meg gets up from the table, pauses for a moment and puts her hand on my shoulder. She looks to say something but nothing comes out. Then, "I've always felt that if a tree falls in the forest and no one hears the sound, it still matters. Thank you for reminding me of this."

6

Can't Buy Me Love

Hitchhiker: Can money buy you happiness?

Larry: No.

(Pauses for a moment)

But it is better to have it than not to. Money can't make you happy, but it can make you happier.

Hitchhiker: What's it feel like to have a lot of money?

Larry: Funny, most days I don't even think about it.

A few mornings later I'm back at Among The Flowers nursing a latte with Billionaire Bob. To the outside observer, it probably looks like we're competing for the *Outfit Most Obviously Bought at the Edgartown Thrift Store* award. Today, in a stunning upset, Billionaire Bob prevails, thus ending my thirteen-day winning streak.

It's not every day you get to sit with someone like Billionaire Bob. Actually on the Island, it's about every third day. He generously gives me a crash course in: politics (Until you change the campaign finance laws you will never see any real reform), economics (1% of the population controls 90% of the wealth in this country), and common sense (If we don't start creating again as a nation, it's only a matter of time until we sink to the middle).

This all feels too depressing for such a beautiful Vineyard morning, so I move things in a lighter direction. "Do you ever watch *Seinfeld*?"

"What?"

"Never mind."

Since Billionaire Bob is so generous with me, I wonder what I can do for him. After all, what do you get the billionaire who has everything?

I remember he showed some interest in my copy of *A New Earth*, so I wander over to the bookstore and pick up a copy. Returning, he is nowhere in sight, so I tuck it away in my backpack. A few days later I'm walking past an outdoor café when someone calls my name. It's Billionaire Bob. I whip out his surprise gift and, to avoid the *Billionaire Lean-Back*, explain that the book comes with no strings attached.

"Did you inscribe it?"

"Yes."

"Thank you, my friend." He puts his hand on his heart. "You didn't have to do this." The moment is both warm and awkward, because nowadays we don't often make a gesture without a motive or Madison Avenue-inspired holiday.

After my time with Billionaire Bob, I bump into my friend Ron. He is an extremely successful attorney who, through years of hard work, rose from nothing to the very top of the legal profession. Trial Lawyer Ron works for drug lords, corporate criminals, and the wayward rich. His legal specialty is getting the obviously guilty off the hook. Though charming, I find it difficult to reconcile what he does for a living. "Ron, what if you focused your intellectual prowess on improving rather than weakening the system?"

"There is no money in that."

"Is money all that matters?"

"It's what pays the rent."

"Wasn't one of Gandhi's *Seven Deadly Sins*, commerce without morality?"

"The law is the law, and I didn't create the system. So why is it wrong for me to profit from it?"

"What about the truth?"

He pauses for a moment. "Look, it's what I do. I can't say it's right, but I'm not sure it's wrong. The world can be a harsh place filled with contradictions. I wish things were different, but they're not." In the end, we agree to disagree and Trial Lawyer Ron slithers off.

I think about the lyric from Pink Floyd's *Wishing You Were Here*…

And did they get you to trade your heroes for ghosts
Hot ashes for trees, hot air for a cool breeze
Cold comfort for change, and did you exchange
A walk on part in the war
For a lead role in a cage

Our conversation leaves me feeling unsettled, so I decide to hitchhike up Island. Before I can even get my hand out, here comes the red vintage Mercedes with Wall Street Mike at the wheel. "You are turning into my chauffer. Do you accept tips?"

"Hop in."

"What brings you to this side of the tracks?"

"I'm on my way back from competing in the Edgartown Golf Club Championship."

"How did you do?"

"Believe it or not, I'm leading after the first round. It's good to see you. Where are you headed?"

"Alley's."

"You are still here?"

"I'm still here."

"Why?"

"I decided to go with the flow."

"How are things with your father?"

"Fine. As long as I'm out and about."

By now the two of us feel like old friends. He drops me at Alley's, and I park myself on the porch. A middle-aged woman sits down beside me. Her clothes are worn and tattered, and she exudes a palpable edge. After a few minutes of awkward interaction, I ask, "Where are you staying?"

"I'd rather not say."

I nod my head. "That's fine."

"Okay, if you must know, I'm living out of my car."

"I'm sorry."

"It's been a tough couple of years. They closed the plant where I was working, so I lost my health insurance. I couldn't find any work and then got sick. I ended up losing everything so I came up here looking for a fresh start. It hasn't worked out too good. Why am I telling you all this?"

"Maybe you just needed someone to hear it."

"Maybe I did. I feel so angry. Like I screwed up or something and can't figure it out. Am I stupid? How come this happened to me?"

"You are not stupid, and you're not alone. A lot of people are out of work. There are six million people just like you, who are homeless in this country."

"Why me?"

"Look, times are tough and a lot of folks are scared. Who can blame them? It's not fair, but people like you have become invisible." She lowers her head, and I'm struck by the contrast between the Island's affluence and her lament. America may have egalitarian aspirations, but every day it feels more like *Lord of the Flies* around here.

"How about you?" She asks. "Do you have a home and a job?"

"I used to."

"What happened?"

"Well, I made a bunch of money in the entertainment business, but it left me feeling empty. Six years ago I walked away. I sold my house, the black BMW, and have been living off my ever dwindling savings."

"Where do you live?"

"With my parents, but considering my dad's mood these days, I may be better off in a car like you."

For the first time she smiles.

"Are you hungry?" I ask. "Let me buy you some lunch."

"I don't want no charity."

"Are you kidding? It's the least I can do for you listening to me ramble." I'd like to be more helpful, but what can I do? Near the end of our time together, I take her hand, look into her eyes, and offer a few words of comfort. "Don't give up. It could all change tomorrow."

"Are you religious?"

"I've never been a fan of organized religion or, now that I think about it, the disorganized kind either. How about you?

"I used to be. Will you pray with me?"

"Absolutely."

Holding hands I feel something powerful pass between us. In the end it's hard to say which of us is more deeply moved. I feel like I am teacher and student, seeker and sought.

I take an old, rumpled twenty-dollar bill from my pocket. "Here, take it. It's all I have."

"I told you, I don't want no charity."

"It's a loan, and I expect you to pay me back. Consider it an investment in your future. Besides, you can't look for work on an empty stomach. It will give you bad breath."

She finally laughs and takes the currency. "But it's a loan and I will pay you back."

"I know you will. Take care of yourself."

I amble along the road for a while before a gigantic crow drops his payload right on my shirt, thus giving credence to the age-old adage, 'Let no good deed go unpunished.'

I pour out my water bottle in a bit of spontaneous clean up and stick out my thumb. A friendly couple in their mid-fifties pulls over and picks me up. "Where are you headed?"

"The beach."

"But you are already wet."

"I had an accident."

"Are you housebroken? We just had the car cleaned."

This makes me laugh. "I think I can make it all the way there. Just don't hit too many bumps."

When we arrive at the Lucy Vincent Beach, my door won't open so I can't get out. They pretend like they are going to leave me in the car with the windows cracked, as if I were a dog. "Don't worry, you'll be alright. It's not too hot, and we parked in the shade. Sally, does he have any water?"

Their comedic timing is so quick, they remind me of one of those classic Vaudeville acts. "So are you two comedy writers?"

"No, I'm heart surgeon." He says.

"I don't believe you."

"He really is," The woman says. "Dan is just a bit crazy." Ladies and gentlemen, it's The Hitchhiking Episode of, *The Dr. Dan and Sally Comedy Hour.* "How about you come to our place this weekend for dinner and let us make it up to you for locking you in?"

In the spirit of the Island, I forgive and accept.

I walk down the beach to an area where swimsuits are optional, strip, and jump into the ocean. An hour later I'm on the porch at the Chilmark Store. (Don't worry I put my clothes back on.) A couple of White-Haired High Rollers ride up on expensive bicycles. Eavesdropping on their conversation, I get an insider's look at the economic meltdown and the ways of Wall Street: "They knew what they were doing and got away with robbery, the crooks are at it again and the government is complacent, and wait until it happens again, there will be rioting in the streets."

The White-Haired High Rollers peddle off leaving me alone with my thoughts. Why must the game be rigged? Are greed and corruption part of our DNA? How come there is so much grasping for bigger, better, and more? Why do some people have more than they will ever need, while others go hungry and live without shelter?

What makes the human collective so oblivious to the weak?

I hop on my bike and take my time winding my way back towards Edgartown. Stopping by the airport, I watch a procession of private jets dispatch and retrieve their exceptional occupants, those gilded few who walk amongst the mortal and common. Like the rest of us, I watch through the links of the fence at the allure of their lives.

The next day at the Chilmark library, I run into the Homeless Lady.

With her hand tightly clasped around my arm, she asks, "What happened with us yesterday? I slept like a baby for the first time in years. I feel hopeful again."

"Who knows?" I shrug.

She's still holding my arm. "What did you do to me?"

"It certainly wasn't anything I did. Maybe we reminded each other of something we had forgotten. I'm happy you're having a better day."

She finally lets go of my arm. "I hope I see you again."

Later at sunset, I sit on a bench overlooking the harbor. A handsome guy with an attractive woman on his arm stops to chat. She wanders off to shop and leaves us to talk.

Doug graduated from Yale and has worked on Wall Street ever since. Like many who take this path, he has become a millionaire. He considers himself an up and coming player on 'The Street' and constantly checks his Blackberry for the next big score.

"Somebody holding your kids hostage?" I say pointing at the Blackberry.

"Forgive me, but I have this huge real estate deal pending in Florida, and I haven't slept for days."

"I'm doing a little research for a book. May I ask you a couple questions?"

"Sure. Fire away."

"Do you feel like you have enough money?"

He laughs. "Not yet. My ultimate goal is to become a billionaire."

"Why?"

"If you want to be a player in the game, a billion is what it takes. This is where the real power lies. I have been a guest in the 'Billionaire Room' and that is where all the important decisions happen. I figure once I'm there, I can do something of value."

"So you need a billion dollars to do something worthwhile? Couldn't you make a lot happen with say, a couple hundred million?"

Dealmaker Doug shakes his head at the folly of my inquiry. "No, not really. Not the big things."

"Okay. Are you happy now with your millions?"

He thinks for a few moments and then laughs again. "No. What do you think about money?"

"It's certainly necessary, but I've always been leery of a monetary definition of success. Bruce Springsteen once said: 'Success makes life easier. It does not make living easier.'"

He nods his head. "Yes, that's true." Though Dealmaker Doug seems to be enjoying our exchange, I can tell it's making him uncomfortable.

"Do you mind if I ask another question?"

"Sure."

"If you're not happy with millions, what makes you think you'll be happy with billions?"

"That's a great question. I honestly don't have an answer for you." He checks his phone again, but still no deal. "Sh—t."

Since this has turned into my Wall Street Education Day among the Philistines I ask, "Tell me about the financial game."

"You have to be on the inside to win, the game is rigged."

Mimicking Captain Renault in *Casablanca* I say, "I'm shocked, *SHOCKED* to know that gambling is going on here!"

Dealmaker Doug laughs and says, "They privatize the profits and socialize the losses so whichever way the wheel spins they win."

"How does one get into that casino?"

"You need to be in the club."

On a purely monetary level, it sounds like a great place to be, but only if you sit on the very top of the pyramid. Still, I cannot find any correlation between material prosperity and the state of happiness.

Maybe Larry is right, "Money can't make you happy, but it can make you happier." Obviously Homeless Lady would be better off living in a cottage as opposed to a Subaru. Would I be any less joyful with a robust bank account? No. Would it have eased the heartache of my breakup? No, again.

What is wealth, and how much is really enough? I don't have the answer to that question, but maybe I'll find it by the end of the summer.

7

Is That So?

Hitchhiker: Aren't you originally from Brooklyn?

Larry: That's where I was born.

Hitchhiker: My dad's from Brooklyn.

Larry: Do you live in New York?

Hitchhiker: No, Nashville.

Larry: Nashville? You should live in New York.

Hitchhiker: (Thinking about it for a moment)

I should?

Larry: Yes, you should.

Hitchhiker: Is that so?

I awaken to sound of raised voices and conclude the *Parental Asylum* is in crisis. Good God, what have I done now? Did I drink the wrong orange juice again? As the

Cabin Scapegoat I sleep lightly and live on the edge. So it is always in my best interest to stay on top of these things. I come out of the bedroom and begin my investigation.

First the facts: my parents only leave the house one night a week. Every Thursday evening they drive over to the old Veteran's Hall for a couple hours of high-stakes bingo at a dollar a game. The competition can be cutthroat and my parents believe the game is loaded with ringers, who avoid detection by disguising themselves as retired old women.

Back to the crisis... Apparently with no regard to the position of his chips, Dad keeps yelling, "BINGO!" The other players clear their cards only to discover the boy has cried wolf. Or more accurately, the wolf has cried bingo. The first couple of times, his fellow players are forgiving. But now, after repeated counterfeit outbursts, they have turned on the agitator. This is scary when you think about it, because nothing is more terrifying than an angry bingo mob.

Here's the worst part: The Executive Bingo Council has decreed that if Dad can't get himself under control, he will be banned for life from his beloved bingo hall. For life! Imagine the shame, the scandal. If, God forbid this were to happen, my parents have decided there would be no point remaining on the Island.

He looks clearly shaken so I offer some solace. "Dad, it's okay." I put my hand on his shoulder, "Maybe you are suffering from Bingo Tourette's Syndrome?"

"Does that really exist?"

"Apparently so. And with catastrophic consequences."

"Oh God." He suffers from heart problems, but this Bingo Tourette's Syndrome is serious stuff.

Luckily this recent affliction has not affected the sanctity of...

The Daily Migratory Patterns of

The Paternal Grouchasaurus

* Get up and drink a pot of coffee.

This allows Dad's enlarged prostate to awaken and start harassing him into bi-hourly wind sprints to the bathroom. After his third cup and fourth flush, it's time to begin complaining about his proctologist. "How did I let that incompetent idiot talk me into that damned useless procedure?" Dad believed this surgery would not only alleviate his bladder use entirely but also bring him a constant state of deep peace. Unfortunately he responds to any suggestion that the caffeine 'might' have something to do with his urinary frequency in the same way that the Catholic Church responded to the heliocentric theories of Galileo.

*Bolt early from the house to beat the terrifying specter of traffic.

He has to pass through a treacherous area called the *Edgartown Triangle*, where the Oak Bluffs and Vineyard Haven roads merge into one insanely clogged bottleneck. Though not as famous as its notorious cousin in Bermuda, it is considered by experts to be even more dangerous. Legend has it that many a moped-riding tourist has mysteriously vanished here, usually between the Fourth of July and Labor

Day. Dad fears the *Triangle* in much the same way that swimmers fear sharks.

*Stop at the post office to pick up the mail.

If it's early in the summer, gripe about the mail not being forwarded. If later, complain about the bills arriving in the forwarded mail. His seasonal shift in negativity is one of the ways in which I mark the passage of time.

*Head over to the Stop & Shop and forage for supplies.

Since he never lets anyone accompany him to the store, his visits there remain shrouded in secrecy. To shed some light, I ask the *CSI: Martha's Vineyard* team to run some forensic tests on his shopping paraphernalia. This is what they found: Suspect only purchases items on sale. There is an abnormally high coupon-to-product ratio. He never leaves aisle five without a box of cornflakes and two liters of Diet Pepsi. The suspect has an odd penchant for unclaimed birthday cakes. (Happy Birthday Yolanda!)

*Return to the safety and seclusion of the *Parental Asylum*.

After managing to successfully navigate through *The Edgartown Triangle,* it is time for some triumphant celebration and a few high fives. The trials and travails of the two-mile roundtrip have left him feeling exhausted, so Dad retires to his reading chair for a long nap amongst his newspapers.

Between the daily trips to the grocery and the overflowing pantry closet, I assume he has the acquisition of sustenance down to a science. This makes my next observation all the more disturbing. About a week into my visit, I notice a subtle shift in his hunting and gathering patterns. After an initial smattering of culinary offerings I prefer, the food that I eat stops showing up in the refrigerator. As a conscientious houseguest, I pick up the things from the market the four of us enjoy (don't forget to count Max). But when my largess doesn't alter any of Dad's buying patterns, I can't help but wonder, if he trying to *starve* me out.

When I casually mention this to him, Dad throws down the hospitality gauntlet. "I'm not sure why, but I don't really like having you around." With this proclamation, I officially add *House Pariah* to my Vineyard resume.

Somehow I ended up on *Survivor/Martha's Vineyard* and just got voted off the Island.

Later, Dad's Personal Enabler (Mom) explains, "He's upset because you don't have a job."

"Was Dad always like this?"

"No, not at all. We spent the first ten years of our marriage living in New York City and having fun. We ate out every night, went to shows, ball games, you name it. He was a handsome and debonair playboy with a quick wit who loved nothing more than having a good time. It was a golden age for us. We waited ten years to have you."

"Do you ever wish you were still waiting?"

"No." She laughs. "When you came along, Dad changed overnight. He became a responsible father. He went out, got a job at the post office and never looked back."

"Why does he feels such antipathy for me?"

"Dad's not mad at you. He's just had a tough life. Remember he grew up in the depression and was shining shoes at the age of four. Unlike you, no one ever showed him any kindness. In fact, he once came home from the third grade and found his family had moved without even telling him, and a neighbor helped him find them. All of this colors everything he looks at."

I sit there and consider this. "It's still hard not to take the things he says personally."

"Never forget your father loves you very much." Mom gets a faraway look in her eye. "I remember when you were a newborn. Dad came home from work while I was nursing you. He sat down next to us, began to cry and said, 'I've never been so happy. Thank you for bringing him into my life. I love you both so much.' He loves you."

~~~~~

Flashback:

I am all of one as my father lifts me up and carries me into the warm Miami water. Surrounded by my inflatable too-bee, I spin like a top until my tiny tank hits empty, drifting off to sleep on the roll of the waves and safe in the awareness that dad is close by.

I'm five and the training wheels come off my bike. I have already taken a few nasty spills. He holds me up on my seat and whispers, "You can do it. I know you can. Ready?"

With fear and trepidation I nod.

He pushes me along, "Peddle...peddle!" For a moment I am shaky, then like the Wright Brother's Kitty Hawk, I take flight on my maiden voyage. I am free.

I'm seven and Dad and I play catch for hours. He is teaching me the subtleties of baseball. There are grounders to be fielded and pop flies to run under. Inheriting his love for the national pastime, we spend hours pouring over the box scores together.

I'm eleven years old and being chased for my life by the neighborhood bully. Suddenly, from out of nowhere, Dad appears to intercept my nemesis. Confronted by an angry, six foot-two patriarch, the villain shrinks. In a deep, growling tone, Dad conveys something menacing. It must have worked, because the creep never bothers me again.

I'm fifteen, and we lay awake listening to the radio. Larry King is interviewing author David Halberstam about the Brooklyn Dodgers, the beloved team of Dad's youth. Dad fills in the details: He grew up a few blocks from where the Dodgers played, it was called Ebbets field, the hopelessly loyal fans were called 'the bums'. When he first started dating your mother, he used to take her to the games. The two of us stay up through the night sharing a love of the game and each other.

~~~~~

Here's my quandary: I want to stay on the Island, but I'm not sure whether 'tis nobler to suffer the slings and arrows of parental misfortune, or to take arms against a sea of troubles.

Or in other words, flee. It breaks my heart to think my father prefers not having me around. But I am kind of stuck; I don't want to go back to Nashville, yet this place is no longer safe. I feel emotionally homeless.

Then my phone rings. One of my closest friends, the Great Simmons, is calling from Nashville. There are friends and there are brothers. The Great Simmons is the best of both. A born contrarian, he constantly pushes me to transcend life's well-worn path. We have spent countless hours discovering and developing our embryonic truths. His wife once confided, "You two are so close, if you were a woman, I would be seriously worried about losing my husband." Fortunately for her, he is not my type.

"How's your summer progressing?" The Great Simmons asks. After listening to me whine about my dad, The Great Simmons shares an old Zen story…

A long time ago in a small village, there lived a wise old monk named Tenzen. One day his neighbors discovered their sixteen-year-old daughter was pregnant. Furious, the parents confronted her and demanded to know the name of the baby's father. Through tears she confessed, "It was the Zen master Tenzen."

The parents went to Tenzen and angrily accused him of betraying their trust. "How could you do this?" They cried out. "You are going to raise this child!"

The great sage listened attentively, replying with no emotion. "Is that so?"

When the baby was born, they brought the infant to the Master's door and said, "This baby is now your responsibility."

Taking the child in his arms, he replied, "Is that so?" He then cared for the newborn with compassion.

As word of the teacher's misdeeds spread throughout the countryside, he lost both his reputation and his followers. This meant nothing to him as he continued to care for the child with great love.

A year later, feeling terrible about what she had done, the young mother confessed to her parents that Tenzen was not the father. Instead, it was the young man in the butcher shop who the parents had forbidden her to see. Horrified and embarrassed, the parents returned to the Master's compound to seek forgiveness. "We are so sorry," they said. "We have just learned you are not the baby's father."

"Is that so?"

"With your blessing, we would like our baby back."

"Is that so?" And with that the Master gently returned the child to the parents.

"Is that so?" These three words become the key to my nascent peace.

Now, in the face of my father's hostilities, I silently respond, "Is that so?"

One day, while strumming and singing, the *Parental Asylum's* new In-House Music Critic (Dad) says, "You should be a listener, not a singer."

"Is that so?" (Okay, wait a minute, bad example. I can't really sing, so this actually IS so.)

It takes practice, but in time I begin to let go and not take his life view personally.

Maybe Epictetus was right, "We are disturbed not by events, but by the views which we take of them."

I begin to enjoy my dad, finding pleasure in even our simplest interactions. He seems to soften a bit, or at least my perception of him does. Either way, everything feels a lot more peaceful.

Late one night I pause to study the beauty of his aged form. How the lines of time have artistically weathered his face like water running over rock. At night I lie in bed and listen to the sound of his voice: the gentle inflections, the pregnant pauses, and the spontaneous joy. Have you ever noticed when people get older, they can sometimes begin to sound like small children? Maybe, as the form winds down, the inner child emerges? Either way, it all feels so fleeting.

Some day my parents will only be ghosts in my life. So I savor these moments like precious jewels.

Is that so...

Sadly yes.

-8-

Ice Cream and Fish Heads

Hitchhiker: Do you ever do any fishing?

Larry: You ask an awful lot of questions.

Hitchhiker: Sorry. I've always been curious.

Larry: That's a nice word for it.

One of the Vineyard's traditional summer pastimes is eating ice cream. Edgartown is ground zero for the finest frozen desert I have ever tasted. During the height of the season, the line at Mad Martha's on Water Street is usually out the door. In an effort to support the summer economy, I try to never go more than a few days without indulging.

After a morning spent helping my parents with various chores, I ride down to Edgartown and pick up a cone. In between my mocha chocolate licks, I get a call from The Hollywood Birdman inviting me to his home for a walk on the beach.

Feeling too lazy and full to bike up Island, I wander up to the Edgartown-West Tisbury Road in search of a lift. My first ride is with a year-round resident named Bill. Apparently he's had quite a winter. He recently discovered his wife was having an affair with his best friend. (Ouch!) Not only did this devastate him, it also hurt his kids.

"Are you okay?" I ask.

"It's been a tough six months, but I feel like I'm finally on the other side of it."

"How long were you married?"

"She and I met on the Vineyard ten summers ago," Brokenhearted Bill sighs. "She got pregnant so we decided to make a go of it. I started my own business and found myself working day and night to keep us afloat. It was a very tough time. We had two more boys, and between the kids and my new company, there was no time left for us. Eventually we grew apart, and she found her way into my buddy's arms. Lately, I'm doing a lot better and feel like everything is going to be all right. Our divorce was final last month."

"I'm sorry."

"Thanks. It took me awhile, but I have forgiven her."

"After everything she did? How did you forgive?"

"Well with time the hurting eased up, and I was able to look at my part in it. Besides, we all do the best we can. We're human."

Brokenhearted Bill pulls over and drops me off oblivious to the impact he's had upon me.   His story hits too close to home, leaving me emotionally uncomfortable. I stand by the side of the road trying to sort through the tangle of emotions coming up from within. What was my part in the knot she and I created? I still feel hurt by the way the Miracle handled things, especially at the end. I feel she could have been more honest. Perhaps like Brokenhearted Bill, I can find forgiveness for both her and myself. (But really more for her!)

I realize that hanging on to the past is like carrying around sharp pieces of glass in your pocket. Until you get rid of them, they'll cut you every time you attempt to move forward.

I take a deep breath, and try once again to let go.

Wall Street Mike approaches in his vintage Red Mercedes, pulling over the moment he catches sight of me.

I bow and say, "What great service!"

"You're welcome."

"Should I start chipping in for gas?"

"I'll run a tab for you."

"That's very trusting."

"I'm starting to think you're never leaving. After all, you are *still* here."

"I am finding the Vineyard a little like the song, *Hotel California*. I can't seem to leave."

He smiles, "Just don't check out. Where are you headed?"

"The Chilmark Store to score a slice of pizza. It's like a cheaper version of crack."

Wall Street Mike laughs. I share a couple of my new relationship insights, and he adds a few of his own. "My wife and I have had a lot of our own challenges. In fact, five years ago we almost split up. Fortunately, we made it through the tough times, and the last three years have been fantastic. Let me tell you this; relationships are hard work, and you both have to be willing to do some heavy lifting."

"Exactly how much lifting are we talking about?"

"Look, wise guy, we did the work, and now we're reaping the rewards."

"By the way, thanks for the ride."

"No problem, I enjoy the company. Oh no, I can't take you all the way. There's ice cream in one of those bags."

"Really, what flavor?"

"Are you serious?" I nod. "Cookies and cream. I'm sorry about the shortened ride." (The guy is apologizing for doing me a favor.)

"No problem. I appreciate the words of wisdom. I hope I see you again."

"The next time I pick you up I'll take you wherever you need to go. Unless it's off the Island."

"Next time?" I laugh and get out of the car.

I walk about a mile along the South Road processing my feelings. I come upon the Allen Farm, a hundred glorious acres founded in 1762 overlooking the Atlantic Ocean. Reaching a narrow and treacherous section of the road, I decide to resume my hitchhiking ways.

A kid in filthy overalls driving an old pickup pulls over. "Hop in."

Climbing into the cab I am immediately struck by an extremely foul odor. "What died?"

"Excuse me?"

My God, how can Pig Pen be oblivious to this mind-numbing aroma? Alarmed, I turn to see his truck bed filled with garbage. Based on the deadly gases drifting my way, I'm convinced at least one of those bags contains a few rotting fish heads. Even the flies refuse to go near this stuff. Motioning towards the bags I say, "There's a mighty strong smell coming from back there."

"I know. I need to get over to the dump and get rid of those bags. I keep forgetting."

Forgetting? How could anyone forget the cloud of stench engulfing this ride? Call me crazy, but even the trees are leaning back as we pass by. I never imagined I would see it in my lifetime: the rare and illusive *Wild Timber Lean-Back*.

Turning back to Pig Pen I ask, "Are you a free-lance garbage man?"

"No, just a chef who likes to fish."

(So, I was right about the fish heads!)

"Where are you from?" He asks.

I want to be polite, but need to conserve air, so I nod.

"Excuse me? Where?"

I almost miss him saying this because I'm carefully calculating exactly how much further I can go without oxygen. I'll either pass out or pass on. As I turn a whiter shade of pale, we mercifully arrive at the top of The Hollywood Birdman's road. I get out, double over, cough a few times, take several deep breaths, and thank Pig Pen for the ride.

That was a close one.

It's funny how easily we can get used to the things in our life that smell the foulest.

-9-

Fame & Misfortune

Hitchhiker: Did success help make you happy?

Larry: Who said I was happy?

The path to The Hollywood Birdman's seaside estate is a long one. I take my time and enjoy the long walk down. When I arrive he is nowhere to be found. I hear the sound of running water and realize he's in the outside shower talking on the phone. The Hollywood Birdman catches sight of me and says, "I'll be done in a minute, have a seat."

"Great. On second thought, it's probably a little early in our relationship for me to see you naked."

He laughs from behind the panel. "You're right. Why don't you go sit on the porch and check out the view?"

I wander over to one of his guesthouses and look out at the sea.

Now clothed he finds me and says, "Do you realize our meeting the other day would've never happened back in the real world?"

"Really?"

"Yes. My life there is too insulated."

"So you never hang out with hitchhikers?"

"Not very often, and I'm already wondering if today is a mistake." He says this with a wink.

"What's it like on the inside of the film industry?" I ask.

"The movie business is a glitzy world of surface glamour with all kinds of serious dysfunction lurking below. Trust me, it's ugly."

"Can fame and happiness coexist?"

"I have never seen it. In my opinion, it's impossible to be both famous and happy."

"Why?"

"Fame is a paradigm where fulfillment comes from the outside in. It's about the self and for the self. Period. You cannot find contentment and happiness through this path. The things driving you to become famous are not the same things that will make you happy. I refer to being famous as "the disease.""

"Do you love your work?"

"Not really. In a year or two I'm getting out. These days it's a lot of effort with hardly any satisfaction. Here, look at this." He lifts his shirt to reveal a series of scars scattered across his body. "Each one of these has its own story."

"Wow, I'm sorry."

"Don't feel sorry for me, kid." Though he doesn't actually say it, I wonder if these are his battle wounds from a life lived in the entertainment trenches.

"Do you believe there is a mind-body connection between your scars and what you do in life?"

"Absolutely. This is why I need to get out, hopefully before something more serious shows up. Knock on wood. It's also why I am so tiny. I have no appetite. I call it man-o-rexia."

"That's hysterical!"

"Not really. Follow me."

We start a winding descent down a bunch of rickety wooden stairs and into our mutual psyches. We eventually arrive at a magnificent stretch of beach. For a moment I envy him. I would love to live here, but decide it's not worth the suffering. Besides, I love to eat too much.

The sun is coruscating off the waves, and the foaming remnants gently caress our toes. I soak up the collective majesty like a dry sponge coming out of the desert. Sensing a sorrow in him I ask, "What has been the defining moment of your life?"

"Do you really want to go there?"

I shrug, "It's your call. I'm right here."

He sighs and looks out at the water. Then back to me. "When I was eighteen, my younger brother, who was sixteen at the time, committed suicide." His voice trails off. He turns away from me and looks back to the sea. A moment of silence drifts by, as a lone osprey passes overhead. He continues, "For better or worse, it has influenced every moment of my life."

My heart sinks.

He goes on, "Ironically, my son is the same age as my brother was when he died. Crazy, no? Maybe that's why I'm too intensely involved in my boy's life. I have tendency to micro manage his every move, and this has strained our relationship."

"It's natural to be overly protective, especially after what happened. Do you blame yourself for your brother's death?"

"In many ways, yes. I feel like I should have somehow seen it coming. But I was too caught up in my own life to notice."

"You were only eighteen. How could you know?"

"God, I wish I could have done something." He shakes his head, and I feel the regret pouring out of him. He looks around and adds, "Funny, I never bring anyone here."

I know he meant this stretch of beach, but it could've been the dark place in his heart.

We walk a while in silence.

The stillness is eventually broken when he pulls out a couple of plums and a small pocketknife. He pauses to school me in the art of plum selection. He must know what he's doing, because this is the best plum I've ever tasted.

Turning back towards home, our roles reverse, and he begins to ask the questions. "Are your parents still alive?"

"Yes, sadly." He looks at me. "I'm kidding. Dad is almost 85 and Mom is 79. They met at Jones Beach in New York when my mom was all of sixteen, and have been married 59 years."

"That's quite a success."

"Well, kind of. I see them more like Tony Curtis and Sidney Poitier in *The Defiant Ones*. Remember that film, where the two prisoners are handcuffed together in misery? Those are my parents."

He laughs. "Do you have any siblings?"

"Yes, a younger brother."

"Are you close?"

"We used to be extremely tight, but not so much anymore.

"That's too bad."

Look, my brother is a great guy. I miss him a lot...and never more than when I am with him."

"You need to forgive him. So, is there a woman in your life?"

"There used to be…"

~~~~~

Flashback:

From our first night together, the Miracle and I are inseparable. Two forms merged into one being. We walk for miles along the shore and never miss a sunset. On one of our hikes, we see two blackbirds flying together in a tight circle, rising and falling with the sea breezes.

They climb and then lock together in a free fall towards the ground, each time pulling up right before impact. This goes on for a while, before they suddenly fly off in different directions. I feel their aerial acrobatics are a reflection of life's mystery and may symbolize my dance with the Miracle.

How long will we have together? Will we share just a few weeks here at the beach and then part? Or will we be blessed with an all-too-brief lifetime?

~~~~

I return from my Del Mar daydream to the glory of Birdman Beach.

"Well, what happened? Tell me about her."

"Here's the short version: she was a gift from God. We had a magical couple of years. I was afraid to commit and took her for granted. She found someone else. It got ugly near the end and I left. Or, more honestly, fled…to the Island."

"It sounds like you're still hurting."

"Only on days ending in 'Y'. Most of the time I feel shipwrecked."

"You need to forgive her and forgive yourself. It's not easy, but it's what you need to do."

"You're really a fountainhead of forgiveness today."

"I like the way that sounds."

"How does this sound, 'Why would anyone ever want to be married? Do we really need the *Wizard of Oz* to give us state-sanctioned permission to validate our relationship? How do you make a long term commitment and still honor the moment?' All that was just a part of my rap."

"Did you really say those things?"

"More than once. What a load of bull. I fooled myself, but certainly not her. If I ever have another relationship, I hope I bring a greater degree of honesty to the table."

"There will be another opportunity, you can count on it."

"Thanks," I say, putting my hand on his shoulder.

"You're welcome." He smiles and hands me another plum.

"I miss being a part of something greater than myself. Of belonging to a larger conversation than the one about me."

He nods and considers this.

I re-break the ice. "You're right about her and forgiving. I'll get there someday. Okay, one more question. Is a man with a beard inherently wiser than someone who is clean shaven?"

He gives me a look.

"Okay, here's an easy one. What **IS** the key to being happy in this world?"

"So that's an easy one?" We walk awhile with only the sound of the waves and seagulls between us. "You have to find your one, true, authentic voice. Then live from that place."

"Like when Joseph Campbell said, 'follow your bliss.' Is that what you mean?"

"Yes. So ask yourself: 'What is my authentic voice?' Find it, and begin there. Then, once you get a hold of it, never, ever let it go."

-10-

I'm Robin Cook!

Hitchhiker: Why the Island?

Larry: I want to be around my kids.

Hitchhiker: Yes, but do they want to be around you?

Larry: Very funny, smart guy. Remember, you still have a long way to walk if this ride ends here.

Still buzzing from my time with The Hollywood Birdman, I leave his estate and walk up the long dirt path to the South Road. I make a right, meander a quarter mile, enter the Chilmark Store, and grab a bottle of water. I show some rare restraint by passing without purchase within inches of a fresh pepperoni pizza. I pay for my agua, head for the door when someone grabs my arm from behind.

"What—the—hell—is going on—with us? I mean—really, this is getting weird."

The Larry Phenomenon strikes again!

"Larry."

"Who the hell are you?" He asks.

"I'm your guardian angel…"

He laughs. "What are you doing anyway?"

"I got thirsty." I hold up the water. Then things shift. "Wait a minute, what are YOU doing here?"

"Ah, just picking up a few things…" In his defense, he shows me his items.

"Really? That's interesting, because I read you were in LA at a television conference."

"Well, I really was. But I got back last night."

"Is that so?"

"Yes, it truly is."

"Okay, I believe you."

"What's going on here with us?"

"Beats me." We stare at each other in silence for a few moments and shake our heads. "To be honest Larry, I got worried when I didn't see you for a couple of days."

He laughs. "Hey, I left my kids waiting in the car. I better get going, but we need to figure this out." We shake hands and say goodbye.

Larry is smart, funny and a bit off center. And he's right we *do* need to figure out why we keep running into each other.

Is there a message or meaning in any of this? Is there a message or meaning in anything?

Or is the Mystery just having fun with a couple of inmates currently doing time in the earth madhouse?

The next morning I'm still pondering these thoughts at the Flowers, when an older man with his grandson approaches me. "What book is that you have?" The older guy asks, pointing towards the table.

"The Richard Bach classic, *Illusions*. It's about the adventures of a reluctant messiah. He wrote this right after *Jonathan Livingston Seagull*."

"Oh, I remember that one. Are you by chance an author?"

"In a way yes, but I hesitate to call myself one."

"I'm a writer too. In fact, I just got back from China where I was researching my next book about Holistic Medicine." He sticks out his hand. "I'm Robin Cook!"

His inflection lets me know, "In the world of books, 'I'm Robin Cook!' means something BIG." Though a lifelong reader, "I'm Robin Cook!" registers a zero on my *Famous Author Richter Scale*. Unfortunately, the suddenly blank look on my face brings him a bit of sag, confirming my suspicion that "I'm Robin Cook!" is someone I should definitely know.

In an effort to recover, I do a little emergency onsite research. "What kind of books do you write?"

"Medical thrillers. I just finished my twenty-ninth book." Then pausing for effect he adds, "most of them bestsellers!"

Still nothing on my end; more sag on his.

Since medical thrillers are not my genre, this last piece of information explains my ignorance. But still, I should know almost twenty-nine bestsellers and the name 'I'm Robin Cook!'

Unwilling to give up on the literary lacunae of the ignoramus before him and desperate for me to realize I am in the presence of greatness, "I'm Robin Cook!" dramatically raises the stakes. "I wrote *Coma*!" (I'm sure he wanted to add, you idiot!)

Some inner recognition is occurring, but it hasn't reached my face yet.

He continues. "We made a movie out of it starring Michael Douglas!" (You moron!)

Michael Douglas? Wait a second, I know THAT name, and I know what movies are too...

"It was a big hit." (You dumb ass!)

Bingo! We have recognition.

Making up for my earlier indifference, I respond to "I'm Robin Cook!" with a tsunami of over-the-top praise. "*COMA*? Are you're serious? *Coma*? *Coma* is one of the coolest movies ever made!" Not wanting to overdo it, I stop just short of yelling, "You Da' Man!"

'I'm Robin Cook!' is visibly ebullient and proceeds to tell his story. "I was a Naval doctor serving on a submarine when I wrote my first novel. I managed to get it published, but unfortunately no one read it. I started researching what makes a book successful, and sure enough, my second one was a bestseller."

The little boy chimes in, "I love my Daddy!"

Oh, so "I'm Robin Cook!" is the father? Shifting gears I ask, "How do you like being a dad?"

"I love it. We used to have a plane, but when we had this little guy," he says, pointing towards the boy, "We got rid of the plane."

I nod and reply, "Of course," even though I have no earthly idea what the connection could possibly be between the plane and the boy. Let me think about this. They used to have a plane…they had a kid…so they got rid of the plane…beats me. But hey, I'm not about to go blank again and cause "I'm Robin Cook!" any more suffering.

With my literary ignorance vanquished, "I'm Robin Cook!" turns out to be a friendly chap. He must also be a terrific father because his son absolutely adores him. "Seeing you with your son gives me hope that I may one day be a father."

"Well, it's never too late. Look at me. By the way, how's your breakfast?"

"Delicious. You can't beat Among The Flowers."

"If you get a chance, check out the Right Fork Diner down by the old airport near South Beach. You know, the grass airfield where you can take air tours in that old red bi-plane? They make a fabulous French toast and it's a nice bike ride out."

"Thank you." We shake hands and they depart.

My friend Betsy arrives just as "I'm Robin Cook!" is strutting away.

"Who was that?" she asks.

"The author Robin Cook."

"Should I know that name?" she asks.

"Wait a minute. You don't know who Robin Cook is? Are you serious? The great Robin Cook? You have never heard of him? You're joking, right? Well, if you don't know, I'm certainly not going to be the one to tell you. You'll have to find out for yourself."

"Okay, okay, I'll look him up," she says. By now she can tell I'm joking, so I recount the whole "I'm Robin Cook!" episode. In the midst of our conversation, an attractive couple seated next to us asks me to take their picture. The man hands me the camera and shares, "We are celebrating her birthday."

"He always knows how to make them special for me," she adds.

This takes me back to San Diego...

~~~~

Flashback:

It's the day before the Miracle's birthday, and she shares a secret. "Part of me is dreading tomorrow, every year it turns into a disaster. There must be a strange kind of curse hanging over me."

The following day, I get up early and sneak down to the corner store. I pick up a hot latte, fresh pastries, and a bouquet of red roses. As I approach the house, she is standing in our bathroom perfectly framed by the wide-open window. With the azure ocean as our witness, she glances my way, and our eyes lock. Then as if on cue, a light, tender rain begins to fall. Through the open window I hand her the bounty and say, "I love you Miracle. Happy Birthday. May the curse be forever broken."

Through tears she whispers, "I love you too. You always make everything so special."

The Magical Girl & The Equine God

Hitchhiker: Wow, this is really a magical ride.

Larry: Maybe for you.

Lucy Vincent Beach (LVB) offers the finest body surfing on the Island. The grade is flat, and the waves here are the most even. It's a private beach so you need a pass to get on. Of course, there are charlatans like me who through a host of tricks and shenanigans, manage to enjoy it on an illegal basis. (In a plea bargain brutally negotiated with the *LVB Gestapo*, I have reluctantly agreed to never publish the details of how to avoid their detection.)

I wander up Island to Lucy Vincent and down to the far side of the beach where a co-ed group is playing a spirited game of nude volleyball. I decide to pass on participating, since the last time I played here, I had a ball spiked on me, which may someday affect my ability to have children.

During my time in the water I have a thought, *all that Is, does so in absolute perfection.*

Interesting.

Exhausted, I call it a day and head up to the road. A woman pulls over to pick me up, and I hop in the front seat. I immediately feel an intense loving presence behind me. Turning around, I see a young girl smiling radiantly in my direction. "Hello, Mister Hitchhiker!"

"Hello, magical girl. How old are you?"

"I'm six." She holds up six fingers. "How about you?"

"I'm old." I hold up no fingers.

The Magical Girl smiles shyly and shows me two stuffed animals. "These are my special horsey friends. Why do you hitchhike?"

"So I can meet people like you."

"Really?"

"Really."

"You know, I live in an enchanted kingdom."

"Are you a fairy disguised as a child?"

"Yes, but don't tell anyone."

"Okay, I promise I won't," and we shake on it.

"I'm glad we picked you up."

"Me too." She is treating me like a long lost friend. In a strange way, it almost feels like we're related.

"I'm on my way to the stable to ride my real pony."

"That sounds wonderful."

When the car stops to drop me off, the Magical Girl hugs me, and says, "I love you!" This small act touches me deeply.

I get out, and wave goodbye as the SUV disappears down the long dirt road. I reach for my cell phone and discover it missing. Uh-oh, it must be somewhere in that vehicle fading out of view. Sh—t, I can't lose my phone. Frustrated, I set off in ambulatory pursuit.

Staggering down the road, I remember my earlier thought. *"All that Is, does so in absolute perfection."*

Yeah, yeah, whatever…

Well what's so perfect about THIS? After my marathon morning bike ride, and miles of walking on the beach, did I really need a little more exercise? I know I'm eating a hell of a lot of pizza, but I could have skipped this part of the triathlon.

I come upon a field with two horses grazing in the distance and pause to lean on the split-rail fence. The larger horse lifts his head, lets out a cry, and makes a beeline in my direction. Are horses territorial? I hope not. I feel an instinctive urge to run, but my body is frozen in place. The huge stallion abruptly stops a few feet from me and stares deep into my eyes.

Neither of us blinks.

All that Is, does so in absolute perfection.

I find myself humbled by the strength of his mighty presence. With two steps, he closes the remaining distance between us. I gently trace my hand down his enormous neck, feeling puny and insignificant in the face of such raw power.

What could possibly create something so magnificent? His majesty reminds me of the Bhagavad-Gita passage, "For one who sees Me everywhere and sees everything in Me, I am never lost, nor is he ever lost to Me."

Heeding an invisible command, we slowly lean towards each other. He rests his head in the crest of my shoulder as I finally feel myself exhale. With my hands pressed tightly against his neck, I feel the rhythmic force of his beating heart.

We share a moment of pure connection as time ceases.

My eyes are closed, and for some strange reason, I see the smiling face of the *Magical Girl*. I take a deep breath. I don't want to let go. I am complete.

Something mysterious is exchanged between us. Suddenly, the enormous equine god lifts his head and cries out. My whole being shudders. We looks into each other's eyes one last time, and he steps back. He turns and leaves me to a world of mortal cares and trivial concerns.

All that Is, does so in absolute perfection.

The Great Mongolian Donut Sage

Hitchhiker: Would you like one of these donuts?

Larry: (Checks out my motley offering of broken pastries and makes a face)

I'll pass.

Seeking fellowship, I make my daily stop at the town bakery, cell phone in hand. (Yes, I retrieved it.) Here, The Great Mongolian Donut Sage presides over his sanctum of donuts and pastries. Over the course of the summer and the expansion of my waistline, the two of us have become close. The good news, I am blessed by our fellowship; the bad news, I can't stop by without wolfing down his donuts. Donuts have always been my weakness. (Along with pizza, chocolate, French fries, cake, cookies, ice cream, pastries, hamburgers, hot dogs, seafood, pasta, steaks, fruit salad, candy...)

The Sage consistently impresses me with his wisdom and humility. He grew up in communist Mongolia and was raised by his grandparents after his alcoholic father abandoned the family. He currently studies philosophy at the University of Berlin and journeys to the Island each summer to earn some extra cash.

"Do you ever see your father?" I ask.

"No, not often. I have a love-hate relationship with the guy."

"I have that with my dad too. I love him, and he hates me." This line gets a cheap laugh and bonds us in a peculiar way.

"We must learn to forgive those who hurt us." The Sage intones. "No sense carrying around the deadening weight of pain."

Between the unwelcome and disruptive visits by actual paying customers to The Bakery Temple, we share our take on life. For someone twenty years old, he is uncommonly deep. Though our lives began in very different worlds, we somehow ended up in the same place, sharing time and tea.

My buddy Big Builder Ben walks in, notices us, and asks, "May I join you?"

"Buzz off!" I say in a faux angry tone.

The Great Mongolian Donut Sage gasps, and Big Builder Ben laughs. "I'm sorry I asked."

"Of course you can." I gesture towards the seat.

Builder Ben sits down with his coffee and dishes the latest Island news. "Guess who I sat next to at dinner the other night?"

"Who?" Replies The Sage.

"Larry David."

"Who's that?" I say, trying not to laugh.

"You don't know who Larry David is? Haven't you ever seen *Seinfeld*? Or *Curb Your Enthusiasm*?"

(I better not go there.)

Like a dime store fortune-teller I cryptically inquire, "Wait a minute (rubbing my chin and looking skyward)...was it...Thursday night? Wait...I'm getting something more...at the Atlantic?"

He looks stunned. "Yes! How did you know?"

At that moment, Mr. Flakey enters the Bakery Temple. "Do you see that guy who just walked in?" I say pointing across the shop. "He will claim to have lost my number and then invite me to lunch. Watch."

Mr. Flakey wanders over and shakes everyone's hand. Then continues Stage Three of his Charade... *Stage Three: We run into each other again, he says he never got the message, claims to have lost my number, really wants to get together, asks me to call him again to set a time for us to definitely have lunch.*

My interpretation: Really wants to get together = Really wants to get together.

Actual meaning: Really wants to get together = Damn, not him again.

Big Builder Ben and the Sage look on in amazement as Mr. Flakey wanders off. Then the Sage asks, "How can one know such things?"

"My friends, I know everything that goes on in this town. Nothing of consequence eludes me." I laugh and then share the truth.

"So you like *Seinfeld* and *Curb*?" Big Builder Ben asks.

"I'm not sure yet. I plan to watch them this summer, but…"

"You have NEVER seen…" The Sage interrupts.

"Forgive me, I haven't..."

"You have never watched *Seinfeld*?" Big Builder Ben jumps in, "That's impossible."

"I'm planning to watch his shows this summer. Now please, can we change the subject?"

They shake their heads in disbelief and disgust.

"Okay," says Big Builder Ben finally relinquishing the topic. "By the way, would one of you be interested in doing a little house-sitting? A friend of mine needs someone reliable to watch his place."

The Sage declines so I jump all over it. "This is heaven sent. I'm sure my parents could use a break from me."

"Great, it's a little cottage right in town. I'll work things out."

It's time to celebrate, so I grab a couple of holy donuts and walk down to the Colonial Inn. Sitting on a sofa in the lobby, I open *Illusions* and am struck by the quote, "Seldom are members of your real family born under the same roof."

How true.

Looking up, I nod to a guy across from me who looks vaguely familiar. We chat for a minute before I recognize him. "You know, the world is a better place because of what you've done."

"Really? What a kind thing to say."

"What are you working on these days?"

"I just finished a film about Iraq called *Body of War*. It was a very intense experience, but it was something I had to do."

"I'll check it out."

His wife, looking as ageless as ever, breezes in and greets us warmly. "It's time to go, honey."

I say goodbye and go back to my donuts.

As they walk out I overhear Phil Donahue say, "That guy on the sofa just told me the world is a better place because of what I do." Marlo Thomas looks at him, turns back towards me, and smiles.

At times life sure can be sweet.

That night I return to Chilmark for The Dinner Episode of *The Dr. Dan and Sally Comedy Hour*. The show's soundstage is a palatial home overlooking the beaches of Menemsha and Aquinnah. Dr. Dan and I take his Wrangler down to Menemsha, the quintessential New England fishing village, to pick up the main course. The dock is littered with lobster traps, fishing lines, and all kinds of other sea worthy junk. Reaching the fish market, Dr. Dan double parks and jumps out. "Stay in the jeep so I don't get a ticket. Oh, and try not to get into any trouble."

"Yes your Medical Highness. Make sure they are fresh." Dan gives me a look that could kill and walks away.

I watch a couple of fishing boats come and go.

"Hi! A tiny voice calls to me. "Hi there! Hello!"

I look down, and staring up at me is the Magical Girl.

She remembered me!

"Hi Magical Girl, how are you?"

"Enchanted!"

"I bet you are."

Her mom watches in amazement, "You two have a special connection. She sometimes even talks about you."

"Really? I call her the Magical Girl." This delights the smiling fairy who has been staring at me non-stop.

Dr. Dan wanders out and asks, "How do you all know each other?"

"Hitchhiking!" Comes the choral response.

"What? That's how I met him too. And now this hitchhiking itinerant has me buying him lobster for dinner," he says, feigning a great deal of outrage. "There's simply no justice in the world!"

Dr. Dan and I arrive back at their palatial soundstage, walk out on the deck, and catch the sun's last gasp before it disappears into the sea. The grounds are spectacular, with views all the way to the Elizabeth Islands. I look towards the ocean, past the expansive yard and the multitude of wildflowers. "This is truly breathtaking."

"You should get married out here on the lawn." He casually suggests.

"What makes you think I can find anyone that stupid?"

"Yeah, you're right. What was I thinking?" He says with a wink. "We always felt this was the perfect place for a wedding, but since our boys don't want to get married here, it all falls to you now." He pats me on the shoulder. "Don't let us down on this one."

I consider if I am up to a starring role in The Marriage Episode of *The Dr. Dan and Sally Comedy Hour.* "I'll do my best Dr. Dan. I'm assuming you and Sally will be conducting the ceremony?"

"Absolutely." Dr. Dan goes inside to check on dinner.

The Miracle drifts into my thoughts. I know she would love this view and for a moment, I wish she were here with me to share it. Recalling our happier days, a feeling of deep regret wells up within me.

I say out load to the ocean and her ghost, "Wherever you are, I hope you are happy. You deserve nothing less." As my thoughts begin to go south, the fog creeps in and surrounds me like a moist blanket. Sweet Sally breaks me out of my sunset lament with a call to dine.

During one of the most delicious dinners of the season, courtesy of craft services, Dr. Dan asks, "So, how's your summer going?"

"Thoreau once said, 'Most men lead lives of quiet desperation.' But in my case there is nothing quiet about it."

Dan shakes his head. "I'd like for you to meet my friend, Livingston Taylor. You know, James Taylor's brother? I think you guys would really click. You're both crazy in the right kind of way."

"Livingston Taylor?" I say. "He is an amazing artist in his own right. I've always loved his music. We actually met on the Island twenty-three years ago…"

~~~~

Flashback:

One morning, during the embryonic days of my hitchhiking career, I stick out my thumb and end up in Aquinnah. After a glorious day on the beach, I walk up to the road to catch a ride home. Within a minute a truck pulls over and the driver sticks out his hand. "Hi, I'm Livingston Taylor. Hop in."

We quickly fall into an interesting conversation regarding the nature of happiness, and Livingston shares his passion for flying. "There's nothing like being up in the air. Hey, do you have time to come by my house and help me move some stuff?"

"Sure."

We end up at his seaside cabin that is more camp than palace. Stopping in front of a huge pile of junk, he says, "I'd like to move this outside."

"Great."

"Wait a minute, the hell with this crap. I say we go flying."

I can't say yes fast enough.

We pull into the airport and board his single-engine Cessna. Within moments we're up in the air and circling Fantasy Island. As the sun begins his colorful exit to the west, Livingston asks, "Hey co-pilot, wanna take over?"

Speechless, I seize the controls and soon like the seabirds I so envy, I am flying. From my imperial vantage point, the kaleidoscope of colors and expansive views take on a surreal quality.

My thoughts take wing to deeper places beyond the scope of the horizon and things I can see.

Can I remain open? Not only here in paradise, but on the other side of that forty-five minute ferry ride? What if I slow down and do less, yet experience more?

My challenge: to remain fearless and say yes. Say yes to flying.

I return to the cockpit of our flying chariot. "Livingston, it feels like heaven up here."

"Yes. We are free."

"How did I ever get so lucky?"

"We both are, my friend."

Though strangers in form, we are brothers in flight.

With time enforcing its inevitability, and the encroaching darkness insisting our adventure come to an end, we reluctantly become Earth-bound creatures once again.

-13-

Nonnie-nesia

Hitchhiker: How long have you been coming here?

Larry: Years.

Hitchhiker: They sure fly by.

The next morning I ride down to the Harborview Hotel for some serenity, a giant Victorian structure from the late 1800's. This grand dame boasts a long front porch filled with old rocking chairs and majestic rambling gardens. This is one of the Island's great vantage points, with the Edgartown Lighthouse across the marsh and Chappaquiddick Island in the distance. It also has fantastic coffee. After a couple cups of black gold, I decide to take the advice of "I'm Robin Cook!" and check out the Right Fork Diner for breakfast.

As I ride my bike towards South Beach, I realize I'm inadvertently heading straight down memory lane.

About a mile out of town, I stop beside a small stretch of non-descript woods and let the Ghosts of Summers Past take me back to my Aunt Joan's small cabin, *The Yankee Barn*, and the summer of 1974, where it all began…

~~~~

Flashback:

Aunt Joan refuses to allow an imagination-draining television set in the cabin, forcing us to interact and create our own fun. My cousins and I play high stakes poker for copious amounts of cavity-causing candy, while the grown-ups drink gin and gossip about old times.

Every evening the entire household gathers in the darkness to listen to the CBS Mystery Theater on the radio. Our imaginations merge into the flow of the story, and the glow of the candlelight. Our spirits rise and soul-dance in the ether of the high cedar ceilings. I lay on an overstuffed sofa with my head resting on my Grandma Deedee's lap as her aged hand gently strokes my hair.

Outside of my grandmother, my best friend is the cabin's official mascot, a Miniature Schnauzer named Nonnie. Written off by the rest of the cabin as a four-legged simpleton, I see the potential for greatness in this literal underdog. Each day I spend hours teaching him a variety of sophisticated tricks. He graciously endures our summer boot camp ("Don't eye-ball me boy!") in exchange for attention and table scraps, though not necessarily in that order. Our routine is a demanding one. We start at sunrise and end at sunset. In compliance with the local canine union, Nonnie receives regular breaks and double treats for overtime.

By nightfall, Nonnie is smarter than Lassie. Yet something is obviously amiss, for by sunrise, the tiny prodigy has completely forgotten every single lesson he so tirelessly learned the previous day. I have no choice but to make a tragic diagnosis. The poor little beast is afflicted with a rare disorder: Nonnie-nesia. (**non**-nee-**nee**-sia: from the <u>Greek</u> Non-Αμνησία The loss of short-term memory during sleep; most commonly found in feral creatures, bats and small dogs.)

As news spreads of Nonnie's condition, a dark pall falls over The Yankee Barn. One afternoon I steal Nonnie's favorite old stinky slipper. Honoring our Rules of Engagement, he immediately gives chase. To avoid capture I circle the sofa. It takes Nonnie only a moment to do the math and calculate that he lacks the speed to catch me. Thus, his quest for victory is impossible.

This time Goliath will crush David.

Nonnie ponders his predicament for a moment, and then purposely walks away. Since he never gives up so easily, this unprecedented act of surrender confuses me. A moment later, to my utter shock, Nonnie returns with my prized baseball glove clinched between his fangs.

"Fancy a little horse tradin', human?"

Oh my God!

This tiny canine, with a brain the size of a walnut, has been scamming me the whole summer. Apparently I am the naïve mark being played for the fool. By 'forgetting' his tricks, Nonnie continually forced us to start from scratch, thus providing himself with a daily bevy of treats. If he had 'remembered' his routine, the game is over and there is no culinary windfall.

I've been had!

This whole time I was merely a pawn in his Machiavellian plot for unfettered access to the abundance of the pantry. I am obviously no match for the manipulating machinations of such a diabolical mastermind. When I realize the inferiority of my intellect in relation to this canine conman, my young ego is crushed.

After sulking for a couple of days out in the woods, a new, deeply-humbled me emerges. I vow to never underestimate the intelligence of any creature (besides man) again.

A Tale of Two Summers

Hitchhiker: What do you do here all summer?

Larry: Work on my show, play some golf, and see my kids... What about you?

Hitchhiker: I was hoping to write a book.

Larry: Really, about what?

Hitchhiker: Maybe a travel guide for serial killers.

I linger by these woods savoring a few more memories of Nonnie and those innocent times: that foggy day at the Wharf when I caught my first fish, the time we gathered up the courage to ride our bikes over to the haunted Dinesmore place, the summer we 'borrowed' mopeds, got caught, and paid a hefty fine. (Never one to overreact, Mom declared that I was on my way to a life of crime.)

I get back on my bike and travel another mile down memory lane. There I turn onto a small side street and let the Ghosts take me back to 1981...

~~~~

Flashback:

It was the best of summers; it was the worst of summers.

The stars aligned to create a perfect storm of decadence and debauchery: the right house, endless days of chamber-of-commerce weather, plenty of piano work, and an ideal mix of cool roommates.

The MVY Animal House

In room number one, Neil and Dave, guardians of a glorious stretch of private beach where we spend our days diligently working on future cases of skin cancer.

In room number two, The Artist Formerly Known as The Musinski`, the ultimate lightning rod for misery and misfortune. The only thing greater than his love of humanity...is his hatred for people. Though The Musinski` lacks the basic social skills of most bipeds, beneath it all, I mean way, way down there...okay, go even a little further... don't give up... keep going... there... lives a great heart.

In room number three, my brother Chris, the hardworking farm hand, and me, the Island's Barry Manilow.

Farmhand Chris spends long, brutal days at the mercy of the plantation's cruel overseer, literally killing himself for a small pittance. He staggers in every night like Jim Casey from "The Grapes of Wrath."

The only discernable perk of Chris's agricultural internment is a daily allotment of free eggs. These eggs, along with Kraft's Macaroni and Cheese (each chemical-laden box carrying a shelf life that can only be measured in light years), become the culinary staples of the MVY Animal House.

Sensing Chris's spirits sinking into a dark abyss, I dutifully assume the role of in-house inspirational speaker, generously providing regular yet obviously theoretical lectures on the virtues of hard work. These talks are usually conducted during his nightly tick-removal sessions, where like a tree monkey, I carefully scan his sunburned body for any pestilence that has mistaken him for one of the farm animals.

After about a month of slave labor, Chris's prayers are answered when he is summarily fired for reasons that to this day have never been properly explained. On the positive side, the MVY Animal House's collective cholesterol levels immediately drop 68%.

Returning to the vocational casino of life, once again Chris rolls snake eyes, winning a dishwashing job at a local restaurant. Ten hours a day he toils at the mercy of two highly creative sadists whose primary goal is to destroy their employees' will to live. For some strange reason, my brother finds working in an extremely confining space, while doing a lot of heavy lifting in 120-degree heat with steam blasting away at his aching body as the hostile proprietors yell obscenities at him, not to his liking.

Go figure.

Playing a Hobart technician proves to be about as financially rewarding as his previous role as feudal serf. Somewhere his dream of a fun and carefree summer has gone horribly awry.

Since my coffers are overflowing with coin as well as guilt, I encourage my brother to resign from the hospitality industry and spend the rest of the summer in recovery on my fraternal payroll.

One evening under a full moon on the virgin sands of South Beach, a few yards from the crashing sea, on top of a nasty old sleeping bag, I participate in life's oldest dance for the first time. With the beaming Luna lurking over my shoulder, she and I rise and fall like the nearby waves. The god's of primal passion fill our forms and overtake us with the sweet nectar of ecstasy. Afterwards, I feel as though I have crossed a river into a new land of brighter colors. In the delightful afterglow of the moment, it occurs to me that every person that has ever walked the earth has arrived through this sacred act of creation.

The state of my chastity isn't the only thing altered that evening; that old sleeping bag is transformed as well. It is henceforth christened The Shroud and takes on supernatural powers in seducing the opposite sex. By August with its conquests piling up, The Shroud begins to achieve mythic status.

This track record is made all the more impressive given its surly aroma. Or, to put it bluntly, The Shroud reeks. (Imagine an unkempt donkey stall.)

When the success and the stench of The Shroud reach biblical proportions, an Official MVY Animal House Council is convened. After much deliberation and even more beer, the council proclaims: "It would be sacrilegious to desecrate The Shroud with something as pagan as soap. We hereby grant Sanatoricus Pardemius, or in plain English, a sanitorial pardon in perpetuity."

Unfortunately, this story does not have a happy ending. In an act of unimaginable negligence, upon my departure I leave The Shroud in the care of the household. (Oh, the folly of youth.) What was I thinking?

As legend has it, The Shroud spent years wandering in the desert and even spent time with a popular entertainer in Las Vegas. It eventually wound up at a fraternity house in the northeast, where one night under a luminous full moon, it magically ascended, never to be seen again.

-15-

Not My Day To Die

Hitchhiker: Do you believe in fate?

Larry: Not really. Do you?

Hitchhiker: Sometimes…

I release my regrets surrounding *The Shroud* and continue my ride towards the diner. Cruising past an open field of farmland, I wonder how this vast expanse of landscape has evaded the developer's grasp. The people of the Vineyard have been vigilant in protecting this Island. There was practically blood spilled when the McDonalds Corporation had the audacity to propose an Edgartown franchise. I'm grateful that, somehow in the land of the bulldozer, the Vineyard has managed to stay so pristine.

As I reach the coast, the Ghosts decide the diner can wait. I park my bike and walk out onto the soft sand of the Right Fork Beach. Of course they would bring me here. As the tide drifts in, my thoughts drift back to the summer of 1987…

~~~~

Flashback:

I am living in the city of 'Lost' Angeles where everyone else is rich and successful while the twenty-six year old me can't even get arrested. Absolutely nothing clicks, and I find myself struggling with depression. I begin to question my existence. "Why am I here? In this vast universe is my existence relevant? Does my meaningless life matter?

What's it all about, Alfie?

As my pain grows deeper, my Inner Vineyard Homing Device kicks in and I instinctively return to the Island. In a bit of good fortune, my brother Chris decides to join me.

One brilliant August day we wander down to the Right Fork Beach to ride a few waves. The surf is raging and the riptide fierce, so the wiser sun worshipers, including Chris, prudently stay out of the water. Being a strong swimmer, I arrogantly dive in and tempt fate.

It takes my hubris only a couple of minutes to realize the water has a will of its own. I attempt to swim laterally out of the rip, but this invisible river will have none of it. Undeterred, I kick into high gear and begin to fight this malevolent force.

I look around and realize the current has already pulled me a fair distance from shore. Though giving it my all, I'm no match for this massive tidal beast dragging me towards oblivion. My body begins to cramp and with no one close by to assist, my inner warning lights begin to flash code-red. I have an alarming thought, "On this sparkling day, a couple hundred yards from the serene safety of the shore, I could possibly die."

My primal survival mechanism screams in defiance, 'NO! I'm not going to die today. I refuse to drown. I will live!'

A silent voice from a timeless, peaceful place emerges and something snaps. I suddenly feel a strange detachment from the fellow in the water struggling to survive. The voice begins to speak... **This is my moment of transition.**

The linear person in the water replies, 'Why here and now? I never got to say goodbye to everyone. This does not seem fair!'

How majestic this moment is. Don't fight anything. Just go with it.

I can't give up. This cannot happen to me. 'I will not die!'

In my struggle to survive, my thoughts cover a lot more ground than my breaststrokes. I begin to run out of energy. Where is Chris on the beach? I have to see my brother one more time. I can't leave him here alone. There he is sleeping peacefully on the sand. 'I love you Chris.'

The last of my will fades, and I begin to rapidly expand out of myself. I can hardly feel my body now. How strange to die. What is this peace? Funny, I do not have any fear. Why?

Time bends, and I'm suddenly ten years old and back in the Everglades National Park. I see the tall grass swaying, feel the gentle breezes blowing across my face, and watch as a deer nurses her newborn fawn. The peace I experienced that day feels like this.

It was there all the time.

I viscerally experience other memories equally as profound...the smile of a stranger, a shooting star, the view from the mountaintop, my dogs' heartbeat, and that extended embrace...These were my moments of authentic connection, when the superficial layers that cloaked my essence dropped away, allowing life and what I Am to merge as one.

All of that exists now in this moment.

My body's struggle winds down to motionless movement, and I begin to feel bliss.

Everything is as it should be.

Looking back I feel a moment of regret that my unconscious actions ever hurt anyone. Yet see it was merely the result of my own ignorance.

There is Grace. Unimaginable Grace.

What in the world comes next? I laugh silently at the absurdity of the question and let go even further.

There is no need to know...anything.

I am finally at peace.

There is so much love.

Thank you. Until now, I was never sure I believed in God, yet I always felt connected to something.

Yes.

I realize whatever It Is… It is ineffable. It exists far beyond words, labels and understanding.

Nothing matters, yet everything is Sacred.

How perfect. Goodbye world.

"HEY!"

Am I dreaming?

"ARE YOU OK? DO YOU NEED HELP?"

These invasive human cries startle me from my tranquil, aquatic ascent into the depths of Being. I wearily look back at the open sea to discover two women on a single surfboard paddling towards me. I find one last vestige of will within and shout, "YES! HELP!" My tank hits empty, and I start to sink below the surface.

One of the girls jumps off the board and cuts through the water like a motorboat. She reaches me and manages to hold me up until the other girl arrives on the board. With their help I climb on, and the three of us paddle slowly towards the shore where we are met by a team of lifeguards.

I'm pulled from the water and collapse into the warm, welcoming arms of the sand. I lay there for a while as waves of relief wash over and embrace me.

For reasons beyond my knowing, this was not my day to die.

Later, I wander down the beach to find the two angels who divinely intervened. "Thank you for saving my life."

"You're welcome. We are here to help each other."

I nod meekly. I say goodbye, and still in a state of shock, walk away. Something within me has shifted. I feel changed, but not in a way I really understand.

A short time later I leave the Island. The days, weeks, and months fly by as life begins to bless me with timely gifts. Ancient wisdom and new friends arrive on a daily basis. Numerous, not-so-random conversations fertilize my embryonic, expanding awareness. Teachers appear in my everyday life: an illuminating read, an enlightening lecture, a class on meditation.

Something wonderful is unfolding.

One evening while reading a book about miracles, I am suddenly taken back to the Right Fork Beach and my rescue from the carnivorous sea. This time I notice a few things I missed...

The two girls came to my aid by approaching from the open ocean behind me. Fine. The only problem is I looked around several times during the ordeal, and there was no one in the water behind me. Trust me on this. When you are fighting for your life, you become acutely aware of your surroundings and there was no one behind me.

I take a few moments to let this new observation settle into my mind, 'there was no one in the water behind me.' But how could that be? At the mind's behest, I replay the whole event and sure enough, it's true. There was no one behind me... and then suddenly there was.

Also, how did I manage to hear them so clearly? How did they hear me? The waves were crashing around us and the noise was deafening. So how did we hear each other?

Lastly, the timing of my rescue was perfect. A minute later, and I am beneath the surface. Lifeless.

There was no one behind me... and then suddenly there was. My mind continues to turn this mysterious truth like a Rubik's cube.

There was no one behind me... and then suddenly there was.

Then, as suddenly as the arrival of my angelic rescue team, I am on my knees, the tears flowing freely. They come in waves, all an ethereal mix of joy, knowing, and gratitude.

I ask out loud to no one in particular. "Why me?"

A timeless voice replies, "Why NOT you?"

"Why do you care about me?"

"How could I not?"

"Do you play favorites?"

"Not in the way you might think.*"*

"Is life better than death?"

"Life and death are two sides of the same coin. Neither is better or worse."

"Can we ever understand these things?"

"Only your heart can know. What matters most is invisible to the naked eye."

Embraced by grace, I fall asleep. Awakened, I am never the same.

16

The Ancient Gods of Love

Hitchhiker: Have you ever felt lost?

Larry: Yes, of course.

Hitchhiker: I feel like I've somehow ended up off the beaten path.

Larry: That's not always a bad thing.

It's a new day and my plan is to take the seaside bike path to Oak Bluffs. When it comes to my sense of direction, I'm more Magoo than Magellan. I usually end up lost. Luckily, on an Island, you can't get too far off course.

There are endless miles of dirt roads on the Vineyard, and I often turn randomly down these streets to see where my tires take me, eschewing the well-worn route for the bike path less traveled. At the fork in the road, I follow a feeling and change direction. I head through the State Forest and wander through her inner confines. Looking up, I see a solitary hawk making long, lazy circles above me. I have no idea where I am, but it's just too pretty for me to be concerned.   In a fitting metaphor for my summer, I'm not lost, I'm just exploring.

I eventually pop out somewhere in West Tisbury. The town of West Tisbury is basically a couple of buildings, the Agricultural Hall, and the store. The rest of it is rambling green space, long stonewalls, and miles of hidden beaches.

Making a left on Old County Road I end up at Alley's General Store.   I walk into Alley's, grab a bottle of water from the cooler and head for the porch.

My legs feel tired, so I leave the bike and decide to travel by magical thumb. An elderly couple in an Old Chevy pulls over and the man behind the wheel asks, "Where are you headed?"

"Lucy Vincent Beach for a swim."

"Hop in, kid."

As I climb in the back, I notice they are holding hands. Ah, lovebirds. "How long have you two been together?"

"Sixty-four years," he says. "I met her when she was all of seventeen, and I was a spunky nineteen."   He turns towards her. "It feels like yesterday, doesn't it?" She nods.

Sensing I am in the presence of something special, I decide to take advantage of this Divine Appointment. "So, what's the secret? How do you make love last? And I'm talking about real intimacy, not longevity, because even some wars last more than a hundred years. What makes love work?"

She goes first. "Forgiving the other person and having a short memory."

Then him. "Sacrificing and not putting yourself first. On top of that, I say, "yes" to everything she wants." He laughs.

She gives him a playful slap on the arm and says, "He has always been a wise guy."

"We love being together, whether it's just taking a drive or grabbing a bite. We always have fun. Plus, she puts up with me and I'll tell you kid, that's not an easy thing to do."

She shakes her head, but you can tell she is loving every minute of it. "A sense of humor–that's a big one!"

He nods in agreement. "You can't take yourself too seriously, and you have to be able to laugh at yourself. Relationships are work, but the payoff is worth it. It's not easy, but it doesn't have to be hard. Most of all, I got very lucky with her."

She beams and I choke up. "Look at you two!" These two feel like The Ancient Gods of Love. "There is a Greek proverb that says, 'A heart that loves is always young.' Whatever IT is, you have surely found it."

"Thank you." He says modestly. "We did, and you will too. Just stay open. Because you never know when magic might happen."

His words hit me between the eyes. *Just stay open. Because you never know when magic will happen.* I sit silently in the backseat and ponder this mantra. This pearl feels like the Holy Grail of wisdom.

Although they look like common working folks, through their love they have found something quite uncommon. Seeing the two of them together in all their glory is inspiring.

We reach the road to Lucy Vincent Beach, and the old rig pulls over. The Ancient Gods of Love let me out and insist on shaking my hand through the open window. It's a tender moment. They are both very old, and I wonder how much longer they have together. How will the one left behind cope with being alone? I hope they leave this world together, like one of those old washer and dryer sets that wear out in the same week. And if love does survive the mortal coil, these two souls will never be far apart.

The Ancient Gods of Love wave goodbye and drive off...still holding hands.

Staring up at the sun I give thanks for the spiritual treasures they have so generously shared. My Helios-induced trance is interrupted by the sound of wings, and for a moment I imagine myself in the presence of angels. I open my eyes and discover I am. On the faded wooden rail in front of me, two doves sit side-by-side sharing space.

As we look upon one another, I remember the last time this happened...

~~~~~

Flashback:

My dear friend Susan calls. "I just left a memorial service for my cousin. He died suddenly at the age of thirty-one, leaving behind a wife and two small children. I keep asking myself, why? Why was this man taken so young? It does not seem fair."

We hang up the phone, and I gaze out the window. Why <u>was</u> he taken so young? I hear a horrific crash come from the front porch. I run downstairs and see a single, beige dove lying motionless on the porch. His rich, red blood is slowly pouring from his head. He must have flown into my picture window.

I notice another dove standing close by. It must be his partner waiting for him to regain consciousness. She stays there at great risk to her own life, for a few feet away my dogs sit surveying the situation.

I step outside to intervene. The hounds jump up, and she flies off landing on a nearby perch where she can still keep an eye on her partner. I pick up her fallen comrade and his body is still warm. I can feel his rapidly fading life force slipping away. I sense her watching us and wonder what she's feeling.

Can a creature this small feel love?

I gently place him on a platform high above the dogs in the brilliant sunlight. I move away, and she is immediately by his side. I leave them for a while, and when I return, she is still holding her vigil. I have heard that, unlike people, doves mate for life.

121

I decide to give my fallen friend a decent burial. I must return him to the earth, from whence he came. Holding him again, I look on his wings in reverence. The patterns in the feathers and the perfection of the design lie well beyond the scope of my understanding. Yet I see in these sacred feathers something larger: the wholeness of life, the transcendence of death, and the absolute perfection of the Divine Dance.

My feathered witness watches as I bury her partner in the property's humble graveyard. I place him gently beside several other creatures, great and small, who have graced my life. With reverence, I put his elemental form back into the womb of Mother Earth and whisper goodbye.

~~~~~

As the doves fly off, I think about the wisdom of The Ancient Gods and their message of forgiveness. Maybe this is the key, but can I let go of that which has hurt me? I recall the Miracle and how compatible we were before things got rocky and crashed. I remember the magic we shared. How we could spend every moment together. Still, I was never all the way in because I was so afraid of being hurt. Yet ironically, my fear ended up creating just that—pain.

I fish out my phone and dial the Miracle. "Hello?"

"I just wanted to let you know I was thinking about you."

"How strange that you called," she says. "I was just missing you."

"Miracle, I care about you very much and miss you often."

"I'm so glad you called. It means the world to me."

For what seems like an eternity I am silent.

"Hello? Are you there?" She asks.

"Yes. I love you, Miracle."

 Silence.

"I love you too."

17

The Ted Danson Principle

Hitchhiker: Wasn't Ted Danson on your show?

Larry: Yes. Did you see it?

Hitchhiker: Uh-well…No, I can't say I ever have.

Larry: (Sensing something)

But you <u>have</u> seen the show, right?

Hitchhiker: Um…which one?

Larry: Either one. You've seen, wait a minute…

Hitchhiker: (Uh-oh… this isn't good)

Okay, first of all, I am not a TV guy.

Larry: You mean...

(I'm busted)

Hitchhiker: I am probably one of five people on the planet who hasn't seen Seinfeld.

Larry: What?

Hitchhiker: And no, I haven't seen your new one either.

Larry: My NEW one? The 'new' one is about to start its seventh season!

Hitchhiker: Oh? (Pauses) Congratulations!

Larry: Are you saying you have never seen EITHER of my shows? Not even Seinfeld?

Hitchhiker: Larry, don't take it personally. I told you, I am not a television guy.

Larry: Now wait...Do you watch movies?

Hitchhiker: Yes, of course. I love films.

Larry: Do you rent DVDs?

Hitchhiker: I'm trying to tell you I'm not a TV...

Larry: (Interrupting) Just answer the question: Do you rent DVDs?

Hitchhiker: Yes. I rent DVDs.

Larry: Then why not get the shows on DVD. After all, why would you deny yourself so much pleasure?

Hitchhiker: Okay, okay...you win. I'll tell you what. I'll watch your show in exchange for this ride.

(Holding out my hand)

Deal?

Larry: (Considers my offer) Okay then, we have a deal.

(We shake.)

(Larry happy now and nodding with satisfaction)

Thank you.

The Edgartown Yacht Club represents a great bastion of WASP tradition. As a long-time closet sociologist, I enjoy watching the navy-blazered bluebloods march down Main Street towards the insulated social safety of their own kind. They may march down, but after a long night of drinking, they usually stagger back.

Since my parents were never joiners, they didn't become a part of the Yacht Club scene. Besides, even if they had wanted to, they didn't possess the proper pedigree to belong. I have relatives on my dad's side who still sport a tail. In fact, when I look up my family tree, I can usually find at least one of them climbing in it.

This morning I'm sharing some conversation at the Flowers with Water Street Wendy. She looks like she was conceived, born, and bred at The Club, though her internal image betrays a blue-collar soul. Three years ago, I shared an idea with Water Street Wendy and she said, "You should meet my cousin, Ted Danson. You know, the actor? I have a feeling he would be interested in this."

I started to pin all my hopes for the idea's success on My Savior Ted, and why not? Ted is smart, progressive, and connected, he would be *perfect* for this. Surely we just have to meet, and everything will fall into place.

Ted, Ted, TED!

So now, three years later at the Chilmark Store, I run into My Savior Ted, who is accompanied by his charming wife, Mary. The three of us share a few minutes together, and while it's nice to see them, something about our encounter feels off. I've always felt uncomfortable approaching others with any kind of underlying agenda. (Obvious Disclaimer: Other than the time I spent exploiting *The Shroud*.) I know we all do this to varying degrees, but I feel better when I meet someone without a pretext.

So while a part of me is now excited to see My Savior Ted, another part feels dissonant. Have I have joined the ranks of those who look to the famous for fulfillment? In our culture, we worship fame in the same way that people used to admire virtue. The celebrities of today resemble the saints of medieval times. So we mortals wish to get as close to them as possible hoping that some of their magic will rub off on us, thus transforming our meaningless lives into something magical, worthwhile and well lit.

I run into Water Street Wendy and mention my encounter with her famous cousin. "Great. I'll call him, and get you guys together. I have always felt like the two of you would really click."

Well, THAT was easy…except it wasn't.

A couple of weeks go by and nothing happens. Water Street Wendy appears to stop returning my calls and acts uncomfortable when we see each other. That's right, it's *The Famous Cousin Lean-Back*.

Disappointed, I let the whole My Savior Ted thing go and give up on my hopes for celebrity salvation.

One bright August day I ride my bike to Alley's for a cup of coffee and the mandatory pastry. Approaching the bakery I come upon The Hollywood Birdman perched on the porch, zealously pecking away at a calzone.

He throws up his wings and says, "Oh, and now you again!"

"You can run, but you cannot hide."

"These days I'm surprised when I DON'T see you. You're everywhere." Motioning toward his lunch, he asks, "Do you want a bite of this?"

"No thanks. It looks kind of pecked over."

"I've got to get home. Does the hitchhiker want a ride, or is it more fun to hitch with the rich and famous?

"Since I'm hungry, I'll cheat and take the lift." I say, hopping into his convertible. "Can you drop me at the Chilmark Store?"

"Pizza?"

"I'm addicted. By the way, thanks for your friendship this summer."

"Don't blow smoke up my ass."

"Seriously, thank you." We shake hands as the car comes to a stop.

I get out and walk straight into the warm smile of My Savior Ted. We exchange greetings, and keeping my priorities in order, (1) Pizza (2) Famous People, I go inside to get my piece of the proverbial pie.

When I return to the porch, My Savior Ted surprises me. "Are you on your own?"

"Yes I am. Are you?"

"Yes, Mary's out of town. Would you like to join me for lunch?"

"I would love to." (The big meeting at last! A famous person likes me!)

About midway through our meal, I realize there is no agenda lurking in my back pocket. I'm just here with a wonderful guy, sharing an interesting conversation. Stripped of any expectation or pretense, our encounter is free to unfold organically. And why should our interaction be any different? Because Ted happens to be on TV? Is that what matters most? Does fame or celebrity give a human being more inherent value? (Actually the answer is yes. According to Wikipedia, a famous person is, on average, two hundred times more valuable than a normal person.)

Ted is comfortable in his skin and exudes an air of warmth.

Ted Danson Highlights

*He accidently fell into acting at Stanford and feels like he got lucky in his career.

*He still loves what he does.

*He met his wife Mary when he auditioned for the film *Cross Creek*. Though he didn't get a part in the movie, a friendship began that led to something extraordinary.

*She is the best thing that ever happened to him.

*God, time flies.

*He loves the Vineyard because there are no high-speed auto chases.

*The Island is truly magical. (A kindred spirit?)

Near the end of our time together he asks, "What are you up to?"

"I'm kind of between ideas right now. The last couple of years have been my time in the vocational desert. But being on the Island this summer has helped clear my head."

In the midst of all this I realize how different my relationships would be if I just allowed everyone to show up and be who they truly are. What if I just let them simply shine their light, unencumbered by the crippling weight of my projections?

Sitting on the porch I feel a shift.

From now on, I will not contort others to serve my imaginary needs. I christen this new paradigm *The Ted Danson Principle*.

As we say goodbye, I officially remove the moniker "My Savior" from the ever-gracious Ted.

18

Mother Nature's Son

Hitchhiker: Do you enjoy the Island's natural beauty?

Larry: No. I need to be on drugs to connect with nature.

Hitchhiker: Ever take in a sunset?

Larry: Nope.

Hitchhiker: Here's some irony for you. I can't get my parents to watch the sunset because they'd rather watch your reruns.

Larry: Really?

Hitchhiker: Yes, they pass on the sunset.

Larry: Well...seen one, seen 'em all.

I usually start each day with a ride along the beach road bike path from Edgartown to Oak Bluffs, and this morning is no exception. On the fourteen-mile roundtrip, I am surrounded by water, with the Atlantic Ocean on one side, and the Sengekontacket Pond on the other. The Pond is also home to the Felix Neck Bird Sanctuary, so the skies are always filled with spectacular aerial traffic.

I pass a few holes of the Farm Neck golf course, and then come upon the Polar Bear Club gathering for a swim at the Inkwell Beach. For generations Oak Bluffs' large African-American population has come to this hundred-yard stretch of beach to congregate and catch up. The town features an array of multi-colored gingerbread houses lining an area called The Campground with an open-air tabernacle that was built in 1879. Oak Bluffs is also home to the oldest operating platform carousel in the world, *The Flying Horses*.

After a long ride along the coast, I park my bike back in Edgartown and solicit a ride. After a couple of minutes, a woman about my age stops and picks me up. In our conversation I discover that she is an international water expert, and I receive a crash course on the world's coming water shortages. Her critical point: "Even if we take immediate action, disaster is inevitable."

"There's no hope?"

"Not really. There will be huge, catastrophic changes in the fabric of the world over the coming years."

"Gee, nothing like a little light conversation to start my day."

"I'm sorry."

"Can I ask you favor?"

"Sure."

"Do you mind dropping me off in front of the hardware store? I want to buy a rope to hang myself."

"That's funny. How about Alley's?" The car pulls over.

"Thanks for the ride."

"Remember, water, not oil, will be the first major resource in crisis. Have a great day."

Undeterred, I grab some lunch at Alley's. I sit on the porch next to a young woman who recently interned on a research ship traveling from Hawaii to California. "Did you enjoy the journey?" I ask.

"I found the experience life-changing."

"Why?"

"There were a lot of amazing moments, but passing through a garbage island the size of Texas," she deadpans, "was completely mind-blowing."

"Texas?" I ask in disbelief.

"Yes. It was gigantic and filled with all kinds of crap. Floating chairs, toys, plastic, and things I can't even mention. Tons of floating garbage stuck together in the middle of the Pacific Ocean. The whole thing was surreal and depressing."

The author and journalist Chris Hedges says, "Cultures that do not recognize that human life and the natural world have a sacred dimension, an intrinsic value beyond monetary value, cannibalize themselves until they die."

All of this bad news takes away my appetite, so I tuck my half-eaten sandwich into my backpack and depart.

After receiving these two devastating environmental updates, I decide to seek refuge at Lucy Vincent Beach. I wander down a long road and come upon endless miles of golden sand. I gaze at the rows of dunes, formed by their timeless dance with the wind. Jumping into the surf, nature rewards me with set upon set of perfect breakers.

I find freedom in the waves as they powerfully propel me through the water. You have to let go and trust the sea, for you are completely at her mercy.

I have never thought of it until now, but bodysurfing is a pretty good metaphor for life.

Looking up, I find myself swimming with a couple of seals. In all my years in the water, this is a first, so I discreetly try to get as close to them as possible. (Kind of like I did with Mary and Ted.) Every now and then the seals stop and stare back at me. Maybe I'm projecting, but we appear to look upon each other with a shared sense of curiosity, though God only knows what they think. *"Who is this strange, poorly designed creature sharing our habitat?"*

I stop for a moment and take stock in my surroundings. Confucius once said, "Always and in everything let there be reverence." On days like this, it's easy. The sun is shining brightly in an almost cloudless sky, and I'm struck by how exquisite this place feels. How fortunate am I to simply bask in this glory, like my shiny black swimming buddies and the seagulls on the shore rifling through my backpack in search of my sandwich.

The gulls finish my leftovers and let out a cry, which I choose to interpret as a gesture of gratitude.

"You're welcome!"

As a child of stardust and mysterious animating forces, I have always roamed the Earth with a profound sense of awe. This day is no exception. Looking up into the deep blue, I notice a rare sun rainbow painted brilliantly across the sky. Is this a gift for me and the other creatures? Perhaps it is a covenant? Whatever its meaning, I know it is sacred; I feel hopeful, even inspired.

The timeless words of Chief Seattle ring through my being…"This we know: the earth does not belong to man, man belongs to the earth. All things are connected like the blood that unites us all. Man did not weave the web of life; he is merely a strand in it. Whatever he does to the web, he does to himself…"

My gratitude overwhelms me, and I cannot separate the sea's salty water from the taste of my own tears.

-19-

The Lucky One

Hitchhiker: Why do you think you were successful?

Larry: I got lucky.

Hitchhiker: Lucky?

Larry: I found a partner the public happened to like.

Hitchhiker: Jerry?

Larry: Yes. He was the perfect person to relay my brand of comedy.

That evening through the grace of my friends, I attend a clambake at a huge estate on the south shore. These mansions exist miles away from the mainstream lives that most of us inhabit. As I wander the grounds I wonder, 'can a person hide oneself from the pain and suffering of the everyday world?'

The cool night air cascades off the Atlantic Ocean and catches up to me on a remote stretch of unspoiled beach. I'm seated in front of a roaring bonfire, staring into the shifting and lifting embers. This primal fire beneath the untamed stars feels healing for my soul. How lucky to be here.

And why is an open fire such a rare occurrence in our lives? In our effort to conquer nature, did we kill off an essential part of us? When did this great disconnect occur?

Long domesticated, most of us now sit trapped in towers with windows that never open in an anonymous array of dehumanizing cubicles. A somnolent hive of drones, we diligently burn away our precious lives on work with no connection to our souls. We've become a standing, or more accurately a seated, army of medicated slaves, wasting away in search of Madison Avenue's abstract idea of success.

Sitting a few feet from the blaze, I feel a force rise within me. Something ancient is stirring and ascending to the surface. Are these Spirits from the past, ready to emerge from within my modern persona? These powerful forces long for a kind of freedom that cannot be found in the castrated world of concrete.

I must get up and move. I take a marathon walk along the ocean's edge and eventually collapse into the dunes. I gaze in awe at the diamond sky, the Milky Way's infinite suns and wonder, 'is there another life-sustaining planet out there with a being pondering these same mysteries?'

"There has to be!" I say aloud to my unknown and distant comrade.

A beam of light travels 186,000 miles a second. The nearest star other than the sun, Alpha Centauri, is about four light years away. I ponder the unimaginable astronomical expanse in front of me and feel hopelessly insignificant. My casual cares and concerns vanish instantly when placed in proximity to such limitless space.

Carl Sagan once said, "For small creatures such as we the vastness is bearable only through love." I wonder if somewhere Copernicus is smiling.

These burning thoughts within me keep the cold sea air at bay. I remember a night like this I shared with the Miracle...

~~~~~

Flashback:

It is a winter evening in Nashville, and the Miracle and I sit in the hot tub on the back deck. The water is a welcoming 110 degrees. Snow covers the ground, and the temperature hovers near zero. Andrea Bocelli's magnificent tenor serenades us from the speakers in our bedroom. A million distant lights fill the night sky with their celestial brilliance. Her back is pressed against me, my arms wrapped around her exquisite form like a favorite shawl. We count shooting stars and contemplate the mystery of being.

Suddenly, just off the porch, something stirs. We turn to see two voyeuristic deer standing close enough to splash. They look at us longingly, as if seeking permission to intrude. How tender they are. We bless them as welcome witnesses to our Sacred moment.

Looking back towards the heavens, a meteor comes to its dramatic flaring fulmination. "Make a wish," she says.

"I did...and you're here."

And we melt into one...

~~~~~

The next afternoon I'm at the other end of the molecular spectrum at an Edgartown cocktail party in an awash of blue blazers, deep tans, and inane small talk. These folks tend to haul around their genealogy papers like most of us carry our driver's licenses. At least the food is sensational. In case you end up trapped at one of these affairs, here are a few helpful hints...

Edgartown Cocktail Party Helpful Hints

*Order a gin and tonic, the ultimate drink for belongers.

*I know this goes without saying, but pretend the people serving you are invisible.

*Never interact with someone new. What would be the point?

*Guys, go with the blue blazer and khaki slacks. Tan pants if you want to really shake it up. Always keep one hand in your pocket and nod a lot.

*Gals, wait until she walks away, *then* begin to gossip about her.

*Throw your head back with verve and laugh dramatically at the old stale jokes.

*You should have recently been in the sun, preferably sailing.

Which leads us to our next section, acceptable subjects of conversation. If these subjects cover too much ground, narrow it down to the select few you feel most comfortable with...

Edgartown Cocktail Party Acceptable Topics of Conversation

*Sailing.

*Will the weather be suitable for sailing?

*What happened the last time you went sailing?

*Your expensive sailboat you are refurbishing.

*Any sentence with the word 'spinnaker' in it.

*Recalling the glory days at boarding school on the sailing team.

*Wistfully wishing you were out on the water right now... sailing.

I leave the party and walk a mile to the Edgartown Post Office to mail a letter. Feeling lazy, I decide to hitch back to town. An old Ford Explorer pulls over, and I immediately recognize the driver.

"Where are you headed?" He inquires.

"Back to town. How about you?"

"I'm just running some errands."

"Mind if I tag along?"

"Are you sure? You would probably be bored."

"It would be nice to spend some time with you."

"Okay son. Can you believe this heat? We should have gotten a place in Canada."

"Yes Dad, you should have. How come it always gets so hot in August?"

I need to take a moment here and point out the broad parameters of *Dad's Comfortable Climate Window*. The temperature should be between 70-72 degrees, the humidity at 43%, no clouds in the sky, barometric pressure holding steady, with a light sea breeze. Anything outside of this zone makes him irritable and warrants complaining. It also inspires talk of preferable places to live with more suitable biospheres. Canada, Miami Beach, San Francisco, North Carolina, Las Vegas…Of course, for this system to work, Dad would have to own at least one home for every day of the year.

As we drive around town, I notice his hands on the steering wheel. My father has soft, beautiful hands with lines weathered and tethered by life. I imagine those hands holding me as a baby. Ah, the passage of time.

Like the film *Field of Dreams,* **baseball has always been a touchstone for** us. "Can you believe the Red Sox?" I ask.

"Take it from an old Brooklyn Dodgers fan, the heartaches never end. Boy, the Island is packed." This next complaint is another annual rite of passage similar to the return birds of Capistrano: "They should limit the number of cars they allow on the ferry."

I fulfill my portion of the ritual and say, "I know they should."

"How's your place in town working out?"

"It's small, but all I really need. The price is right: it's free."

"Are you taking care of yourself?"

"Yes and no. Despite my appearance I haven't gone completely feral. A friend works down at the bakery, and he's always plying me with free donuts. Did you see the article in last week's Vineyard Gazette about me being on track to break my own record for 'the most donuts consumed in a single month?' I guess we all have to be good at something. Eating must be my calling."

He laughs. "You don't look like you've put on any weight."

"If I wasn't riding my bike all over the Island, I'd be visible from space. This has been a great summer for indulging my pagan passions."

"Are you still doing a lot of hitchhiking?"

"All the time. I sometimes feel like writing a play called, *Death of a Hitchhiker*. I would play the hitchhiking Willy Loman, 'a man way out there in the blue, riding on a smile and a shoeshine.' Though I'm usually wearing sandals and someone else is doing the driving."

"Maybe Larry David will pick you up again."

"I doubt it. Not after all the questions I asked him the last time. I'm sure if he saw me again, he would pass me by."

He smiles. "Hitchhiking doesn't seem out of place here. In fact, it's part of the charm of the place. I've even done a little of it myself."

"What?" This is a new revelation. "Dad, you're kidding. When?"

"About ten years ago. The car was in the shop for a week, so it was the only practical way to get around. I found it easy to get a ride and to be honest, I really enjoyed myself."

Like father like son.

"You were a seventy-five year old hitchhiker?"

"Yes."

"So when I look at you, I see my future?" (Oh God...)

"In more ways than one, Son." He's probably right. "The apple never falls far from the tree."

"Dad, it's nice to finally talk."

He pats me on my leg. "It's funny, but we have probably spoken more on this ride than I ever did with my own father."

"Really?"

"He left early, and I never saw him much after that." He shakes his head. "I remember so little about him."

"I'm sorry." I feel like I just had the wind knocked out of me. Putting my hand on his arm I say, "I appreciate everything you did. Thank you. I am truly the lucky one."

"We do the best we can."

The next few minutes pass in silence, as the smell of jasmine and sadness hang helplessly in the humid summer air.

We finish up our errands, and he drops me in town. I kiss him on the cheek and whisper, "I love you, Dad."

He starts to pull away and then stops. "You should come out and see us. We miss you."

"I'll ride out soon. I've missed you too. Give Mom my love. Oh, and Dad, thanks for the ride."

"You're welcome." He hands me an apple. "Oh, here."

"In lieu of a donut?"

He smiles. "It's good for you." This small act touches a deep place within. And with that, Dad drives off, ending our only one-on-one interaction of the summer.

It feels strange to come across my father so randomly. Though the two of us live within a mile of one another, we exist in parallel universes. I picture myself in his shoes: I'm near the end of my life and my son is close by, yet I'm completely indifferent to his existence. I search my soul for empathy, but come up empty-handed.

It's hard to face, but in the world of my dad, it feels as though I don't really matter.

Have I become the Vineyard Telemachus, searching in vain for his absent father? I wander down to the waterfront and sit with this a while. I think about all the father figures I have been meeting, and the qualities they embody that inspire admiration. Can I somehow find the light within my own?

A few observations bubble up within me…Dad may not be wealthy or famous, but he has integrity. He's always been a humble, stand-up guy. A brilliant man, with one of the sharpest minds I have ever encountered. He served in the United Stated Army Air Corps during the Second World War in exotic locales like India, Burma, and China. Did he once have a great passion? Mom once mentioned that Dad had been the lead in all the school plays and had considered pursuing an acting career in Hollywood.

What happened?

What were his dreams?

The answers to these questions remain as mysterious to me as the source of my own being. It saddens me that I seem so incapable of reaching him.

As the fog creeps across the harbor, I hold the apple tentatively between my hands, and then slowly take a bite.

Racial Evolution

Hitchhiker: Larry, what brings you the most satisfaction?

Larry: When I discover a really great idea and start developing it.

Hitchhiker: This is number one?

Larry: (Thinking for a moment) And making a woman laugh.

(Pauses) What is that about?

Hitchhiker: It probably goes back to the caveman comedians, where only the funny would survive. I mean, think about it. This certainly gives a whole new meaning to dying onstage.

A few nights later I am on a bench at the corner of Water Street and Main listening to Troubadour Dave sing and play his guitar. More stylist than purist, he moves me with his unique interpretations of the classic and obscure.

Between tunes, the old minstrel regales me with his theories on everything from the Illuminati to UFO abductions.

"Have you seen the latest crop circles with the Fibonacci Code in them?"

"I have not."

"Check it out, it will blow your mind." And with that he starts his second set. As the songs roll off his tongue, I watch the human genome parade stroll by. What a scene. 'Dave, this is truly the greatest show on Earth.' The people are out in droves, and they're not the only species walking the streets. The skunks are roaming about too.

That's right, the skunks!

According to Vineyard legend, an Island politician angry over a lost election, decided to extract revenge on the locals. He introduced the stinky creatures to the Island, talk about the foul smell of politics. Now the skunks are everywhere. I hold my breath as the striped creatures pass within a foot of me. (I have yet to be sprayed.) Hey, who said humans and animals cannot co-exist?

I start talking to a guy who I realize is Henry Louis Gates, the Harvard Professor who recently rose to fame when he was mistakenly arrested in his own home. (Believing Dr. Gates posed a threat, the police handcuffed him and carted him off. Later, in a courageous effort to move race relations forward, President Obama invited Dr. Gates and the arresting officer to the White House for a groundbreaking photo-op.

Dr. Gates is charming, witty, and warm. He also limps severely, walks with a cane, and is VERY small. I'm talking tiny.

In the midst of our conversation, I inadvertently chuckle at the absurdity of this person posing a threat to anyone, let alone, four large, armed police officers. When he looks at me strangely, I explain my laughter and add, "I think you handled your recent confrontation extremely well."

"Thank you. I appreciate that." He replies. "You should come to my racism symposium at the Whaling Church. We have a terrific panel this year."

"I would be honored." We say goodbye, and I watch him hobble off down Water Street.

The next morning at the Flowers, I have an idea. I could interview Dr. Gates about the evolution of race relations and have it published in the Vineyard Gazette. Five minutes later, fate lends a helping hand when my buddy Big Builder Ben introduces me to Julia Wells, the editor of the Vineyard Gazette. (I love it when stuff like this happens!)

Julia agrees to print the piece if it lives up to the paper's lofty standards.

They depart, and I go back for a French Roast refill. While waiting in line, I meet an interesting women who informs me this is her first visit to the Vineyard, so I help her with a few insider tips. I take my latte out into the garden to plot my next move. (On Dr. Gates, not the woman!)

The woman wanders out and asks, "May I can join you?"

"Please."

Eventually we get around to introductions, and with typical Island informality, no last names are given. We share a fascinating conversation about her experience as an activist and an artist. It doesn't take me long to realize I am in the presence of someone special. "When it comes to race, do you feel as society we are evolving?"

"In some ways yes, and in some ways no. As an African-American, I can tell you we still have a long way to go."

"What type of work are you involved in?"

"I'm an actress. For a long time I was on the television show ER. Have you seen it?"

"No, I missed that one. So I am oblivious to your fame and misfortune."

She laughs. "I could tell. Interacting with a person who knows me based on celebrity is much different than someone approaching me cleanly. I prefer to meet someone who is unfamiliar my work. Then, I feel like they're enjoying me for who I really am."

"Who said I was enjoying you?"

"You're funny."

"Not really. Though you should hear me sing. Do people usually recognize you?"

"All the time and believe me, it gets old fast. Hey, I better go. It's my last day and I have a ferry to catch."

I stand up. "It was an honor." We hug and she departs.

A few minutes later, I overhear two middle-aged white guys talking about a black family walking by. "There sure are a lot of 'them' around town this year. They have been feeling pretty uppity since Obama announced he was going to come here. I wish they'd all stay in Oak Bluffs where they belong."

I want to turn around and confront these Neanderthals, or at least throw some hot coffee on them, but what would be the point? I'm sure this guy has a bumper sticker on his truck that says "Practice random acts of stupidity."

How can people think this way? How did we devolve to a place where skin pigment is so important? Now, if someone acts like an asshole THAT would matter, but their skin tone is irrelevant.

Maybe I'll never understand these things.

I decide to go down to the Bakery Temple and seek solace from the Sage and continue my donut jihad. As I enter the Baking Temple, the Sage says sarcastically, "What a surprise to see you here."

I bow. "Greetings Great Mongolian Donut Sage. Master, would you care to join me next week at the Racial Forum?"

"That event sold out weeks ago," the ever-informed sage shares. "You need a ticket to get in. Unfortunately, no more remain."

"Maybe we can crash it?"

He hands me a couple cinnamon-sugar masterpieces. "That would not be wise. Surrender your fate to the Ticket Gods, and hope for the best." The Great Sage smiles and slowly bows.

That night I'm sitting on a bench in Edgartown when my brother calls. We spend a few minutes catching up and then he asks sarcastically, "Have you seen your friend Larry David lately?"

"Actually I haven't, and this concerns me."

I glance down the street, and low and behold, what do you think is walking my way?

That's right: *The Larry Phenomenon!*

"Chris, I know you won't believe it, but in this very moment Larry is walking straight towards me!"

"No he's not. Quit playing with me."

"I'm totally serious. Here he comes…and…"

"Hey Hitchhiker, how's it going?" We shake hands.

"Great Larry, and you?"

"I can't complain. Have a good night, I'll see you around." And with that, *The Larry Phenomenon* moves on.

There is silence on the other end of the phone. Finally my brother says, "That is really weird. What the hell is going on with you guys?"

"I have no idea. But it's certainly interesting. That reminds me, I promised to watch his show."

"Wait. You mean, after all of this you still haven't watched his stuff?"

"No. The weather's been so…well, anyway…it's the summer…and… look, I gotta go." And I hang up.

The next day at the Harborview Hotel, I meet an older man wearing a 2002 World Series Championship Ring. Given his imposing physique, I assume he's a former player. In the middle of our amiable chat, someone walks up and says to him, "I really love your acting."

"Oh, so you do a little acting on the side?" I ask.

He laughs and says, "No, the acting is my main thing. I've been in the field now for... (He thinks for a minute)...about forty years."

(Uh-oh)

"In fact, one year I even won an Academy Award." He says with a wink.

I pause to ponder this...and then say somewhat sheepishly, "Ahhh...You won an Academy Award?"

"Yes. I won it for my work in the film *An Officer And A Gentleman.*"

"And I call myself a film buff. I'm sorry Louis, I didn't recognize you."

Louis has serious charisma, and I get the feeling, despite his age, that he could easily kick my sorry little didn't-even-know-it-was-Louis-Gossett-Junior ass. Fortunately for me, not once during our entire conversation does he get in my face and scream, "Don't eyeball me boy!"

"Louis, didn't you start a non-profit organization called *Erasism?*"

"Yes, I did and I am really proud of that. I've been to South Africa and met with Nelson Mandela and also have a warm friendship with Archbishop Tutu."

"Do you think race relations are evolving?"

"Absolutely. But we still have an awful lot of work to do."

I say goodbye to Louis and then make a few detective calls to find out where Dr. Gates is staying. It turns out he is renting a home in Oak Bluffs, so I drop off a request for us to meet. Hoping it might help matters I include my interview with the late, great columnist Carl Rowan…

~~~~~

Flashback:

I am working on a book called 'What Matters Most' and hope to get an interview with the prestigious columnist, Carl Rowan. He served under President Kennedy before going on to a distinguished career in journalism. In 1999 the National Press Club honored him with a Lifetime Achievement Award.

Unfortunately, no matter how many times I try, Carl's assistant Pam firmly replies, "I'm sorry. Mr. Rowan is just not interested."

One day, completely out of the blue, I feel a strong urge to pick up the phone and call Carl's office. I try to ignore it, but it won't go away. I finally relent and dial the number, fully expecting to hear Pam's familiar voice cordially blowing me off.

Instead, this time a man comes on the line. "Hello?"

Startled, I scramble. "May… I speak to… Mr. Rowan?"

A surly voice replies. "This is he."

Oh my God, it's the Man. Stunned, I introduce myself and explain the nature of my request.

He listens politely and before replying, "I'm sorry. I'm seventy-four years of age and I'm feeling tired. I don't want to do any more interviews."

I press on. "But Carl, I'm ready to get on a plane and fly all the way to Maryland to find out what you believe matters most. Can't you give me sixty minutes of your time? (Long pause) If not, quite honestly, you may not be the kind of person who belongs in the book."

Holy sh—t! What did I just say? There is a deafening silence on the other end of the line. Did he hang up? A few moments pass…still more silence. "Hello? Carl?"

"I'm here…(Silence). All right, I'll do it. Call Pam down at the office and tell her I said to set this up."

"Your office?"

Yes, this is my home. By the way, how did you get my unlisted number?"

This throws me off since I only had his office information. "I…"

"Well, however you did it, I appreciate your persistence. You should be a reporter." He chuckles and hangs up.

Two weeks later, I'm sitting in Carl's living room conducting our interview. Near the end of our long session, we come to a pivotal moment in his life. A sharecropper's son, Carl was the first person in his family to graduate from high school. He then went on to attend Tennessee State University in Nashville. After his first semester at TSU, he could not afford the twenty dollars required for the next term's tuition. So, defeated, Carl decided to return to the farm, his dream of a better life over.

As he walked through the bus station to catch a coach back to nowhere, something guided him. "Turn around and look on the ground. There, littered amongst the green transfer slips, will be the twenty dollars you need to continue your education." He hesitated and the message came again. This time Carl went back, looked down, and sure enough, there was the money. Picking it up, he returned to college and went on to make history.

The world changed because of this small act.

"So, what do you make of this?" I ask.

"I know where you're going with this. You want me to say there's a Divine Plan or some deity made it all happen. What a load of horse crap! All I know is a person lost the money, and I was lucky enough to find it. Case closed."

"Carl, I'm not saying it magically appeared. But what 'guided' you to turn around and look down? How do you explain that?"

He looks stunned.

I repeat, "What guided you?"

His eyes dart back and forth as his mind searches for a practical answer. "Well, I suppose…it probably…I…" Then, like a small child, Carl stares directly into my eyes.

I gaze back.

Suddenly his tears burst forth. I reach across the imaginary divide and take his hands in mine. He leans forward weeping, and I put my arms around him.

The moment is timeless.

A few months later, I pick up a paper and see the headline, "Legendary Columnist Carl Rowan Dead at 75." Thank you, Carl.

-21-

Surreality

Hitchhiker: What's it like to make it really big?

Larry: Who said I made it big?

Hitchhiker: That's true, it's only television...

Larry: Hey there...

Hitchhiker: Seriously though...

Larry: It's a hard thing to describe, it is kind of surreal.

Hitchhiker: Even after all this time?

Larry: (Nodding)

Yes, I'm not sure it ever completely sinks in.

It's the day of the Racism Forum and I still don't have any tickets. I deal with my disappointment by riding to Chilmark on the back roads. I peddle past fields full of wildflowers, working farms, undisturbed ponds, and scenic overlooks. I smell jasmine and honeysuckle as the surreal beauty of the Vineyard feeds me.

Reaching Beetlebung Corner in Chilmark, I have a decision to make: Do I ride further to Aquinnah for a swim, or head back to Edgartown for the event even though I don't have tickets? With the temperature a brutal ninety-four degrees, the prospect of jumping in the ocean is a lot more appealing than sitting on a wooden pew listening to people rail about prejudice.

Some cool comfort or a scorching hot topic? I go with the heat and decide to take a chance on the event. Why? I feel guided to go, even though there's an excellent chance I may ride twenty miles just to stand outside in the heat, daydreaming about the ocean.

About half way back to Edgartown, I pull into the West Tisbury Library for a pit stop. As I enter the building, Librarian Beth is holding a poster promoting the Racism Forum.

Pointing at the poster I comment, "That looks like an interesting event."

"Are you planning to attend?"

"No. I'd love to go, but it sold out weeks ago."

"Well, I have two tickets right here," she says holding them up. "And you're welcome to both of them."

"You have two tickets for me? Really, just like that?"

"Just like that." Librarian Beth hands me the tickets. "Please, be my guest"

"This feels surreal."

She smiles and says, "It is. Enjoy the event."

Sometimes when we least expect it, our tickets show up and we get to see the show...

~~~~

Flashback:

It's my 25th *birthday and my brother and I are making a pilgrimage to see Paul McCartney. His show is sold out and we are ticketless, but that doesn't dampen our spirits. We shall overcome.*

Along the way we travel back in our Beatles Time Machine. "Chris, do you remember as kids riding our bikes to Woolworths to buy our first Beatles record?"

"Yes, and lying on the bedroom floor for hours listening..."

"To their masterpieces..."

"And sharing our souls."

It occurs to us that most of our lives have been connected to their music.

We pull into a parking lot about a quarter mile from the arena. Before we are even out of the car, a guy approaches us and asks, "Do you guys need tickets?"

"Yes!"

"I have two in the tenth row. You can have them for half the face value."

Stunned, we accept. "Chris can you believe how easily we nailed that one?"

"This is so supposed to happen."

As we approach the venue, we notice the tickets have a date from months ago. Chris says, "We've been duped!"

"We should have been paying attention. That was naïve of us, half-price tickets in the tenth row," I say, shaking my head. "Now what?"

"Should we throw them away?"

"No. Let's try to walk in and see what happens."

We casually wander over to the turnstile trying to appear legit, the lady takes our tickets, examines them closely, and says, "You two have fabulous seats near the stage. Enjoy the show." With this bit of news, our anticipation levels climb to epic heights.

Jumping for joy I exclaim, "This was destined! We did it! We did it!"

"PAUL MCCARTNEY!"

Before we know it, the magical Beatle is in front of us, catapulting our goose bump meters off the charts. Near the end of the show, McCartney launches into his spiritual anthem "Let It Be." The experience turns surreal when I take Chris's hand as we sway and sing along at the top of our lungs.

"Whisper words of wisdom, let it be…"

~~~~

Leaving the library I realize I only have ninety minutes to bike ten miles, shower, and get me to the church on time. I call The Great Mongolian Donut Sage and exclaim, "I got two tickets to the forum!"

"Larry David?"

"No."

"Another miracle?"

"Yes! Meet me at the Whaling Church at 5:30 and I will fill you in on the details."

I defy the laws of time and make it to the front door right before the program commences. With the Sage in tow, I collapse into a pew and begin to soak up the positive energy.

Our entertaining host Dr. Gates reflects on his recent tribulations with wisdom and humor. "I believe everything happens for a reason. It's important when we are given lemons to make lemonade."

The theme of the event: 'In light of an Obama presidency, have we reached a post-racial society?' In light of reality, I find the question rhetorical to the point of absurdity. As Martin Luther King Jr. once said, "Injustice anywhere is a threat to justice everywhere."

Thinking about Dr. King and his beautiful prose I begin to daydream and for some reason, I'm reminded of the last few lines of Don McLean's masterpiece, *Vincent*.

> *"Now I think I know what you tried to say to me.*
> *And how you suffered for your sanity,*
> *And how you tried to set them free.*
> *They would not listen, they're not listening still,*
> *Perhaps they never will..."*

Taking my inner temperature, I feel a bittersweet mix of emotions. I look out through the window at a glorious old tree. A deep sadness rises up within me; there is so much hatred and pain in the world. Yet there also exists a great wellspring of love. We do face enormous challenges, but we gather today like a human rainbow to address them. This small act gives me hope.

In this immense sea of suffering, there are islands of great joy. In fact I live on one.

Looking upon the people around me, it is clear that despite our superficial differences, in the end we are very much alike.

Invitations

Hitchhiker: Hey, why don't we have lunch sometime? My treat.

Larry: No.

I sit on the Harborview porch savoring a cup of Columbian dark roast. As the sky sparkles, a magnificent yacht passes by. I think about my friends, Emily and Sam, who live on a sailboat in the outer harbor. Maybe I should give them a call. I would love to get on the water again and go sailing.

A distinguished looking man passes by and says hello. It takes me a moment, but I recognize him as Claude Steele, Columbia University's new Provost, and a member of last night's forum panel. We discuss the pros and cons of yesterday's event and exchange a few ideas regarding institutional racism and education.

After Claude walks away, the guy next to me turns around and asks, "I say, chap, are you quite serious about what you said? You want to do away with our beloved private schools? No serious man would say that; in fact, a gentleman wouldn't even think such nonsense. People will say you're mad!"

"But I am," I reply.

This makes him chuckle. "Forgive me, lad, if I sound a bit harsh, but you certainly *sounded* insane back there." He shakes his head and mumbles, "Doing away with private schools. Poppycock!"

"You must have missed the part when I said 'This would never happen, but...' Anyway, who are you?"

He stands up and presents himself. "Phillip J. Howell IV at your service." He shakes my hand firmly and formally, as only someone saddled by the weight of a name with numbers would do.

I decide to meet him on his own terms. "Not to pry, old boy, but are you any relation to that chap Thurston Howell III?"

"Ah, so you're a smartass too?"

"I'm only being sporting with you, my good man."

Phillip the IV shares his story. "I was an attorney who wanted to make a difference in this bloody world, so I went to Washington to work on Capitol Hill. Over the years I served loyally on the staff of three different senators, but eventually I grew disenchanted by the degree of corruption permeating the system. So I left. I invested in real estate and luckily, I've done fairly well." He looks at his watch and says, "Good heavens, I'm dreadfully late! I'm on the books at ten sharp to meet a dear friend for brunch." He stands up and buttons his blue blazer. "What a stunning day, the wind is full on. I hope I'm not being too forward, but do you happen to fancy a good sail?"

"I'm not very skilled, but it never keeps me from enjoying myself on the water."

"Do you see that boat?" He points towards the harbor. "The one with the blue hull right down off the dock?"

"Yes."

"She's my pride and joy," he says, literally beaming. "She's a vintage Hinckley, the real deal, and I've had her completely restored. Look at her lines in the water. I don't know how anyone can tolerate sailing in those new fangled fiberglass travesties. What do you say we take the old girl out for a proper spin tomorrow afternoon off Chappy and continue this delightful conversation?"

"That's a *smashing* idea, old boy!"

"Meet me at the yacht club launch when the bell chimes three. We'll have a proper sail, then celebrate with a cocktail at the club."

"Gin and tonics?"

"Of course!"

"I'll bring my blazer."

"Right—o! I look forward to seeing you there." We seal our date with another firm handshake. Then, with a strong sense of purpose, Esquire Phillip J. Howell IV, the scion of the much-maligned Thurston Howell III Dynasty, marches off.

Well, it didn't take long for my sailing request to come through. Thank you, Poseidon.

I begin to write in my journal when a woman asks, "Excuse me, would you mind watching my suitcase for a moment while I step inside the lobby?"

"Has the bag been in your possession the entire time, and did you pack it yourself?"

She laughs. "Is that a yes?"

"Of course. Take your time."

When she returns, she sits down next to me. "This place is so beautiful. It's my first time here, and I can't wait to come back."

"What brought you to the Island?"

"I came to attend an event my boss was hosting."

(I know where this is going.) "Really? Who is your boss?"

"Dr. Henry Gates."

I share my story about meeting Dr. Gates, the possible interview, the magic tickets, and my need to get in touch with him to follow up.

"Well, I have his e-mail," she says. "Let me give it to you."

What's going on here? Does the Island have a lottery? Wait a minute, it does: it's called *My Summer* and I already won.

I walk down to the library and e-mail Dr. Gates a short note. Within five minutes, I receive a personal reply graciously declining my request. He plans to spend the remainder of his time on the Vineyard relaxing and recovering. Though technically rejected, I feel no trace of disappointment.

You can't win 'em all.

Nevertheless, I'm amazed at the speed in which these magical things are manifesting around me. As I consider this, the wise words of The Hollywood Birdman ring in my ears. "You are in a very strong place of attraction right now, so be extremely conscious of what you choose to create."

This makes my next choice all the more interesting.

Perhaps in a subconscious effort to remain humble and discourage any attempt to walk on water, I take a ride out to see my parents. It's been a while since I've been to the *Parental Asylum*, and I'm sure they would love a visit from their first-born child.

Peddling along the bike path I try to imagine their level of excitement upon the return of their prodigal son. With 1 being "Why the hell are you here?" and 10, "Look Honey, the Chosen One has returned to save us!"

My guess is it will be…probably around a seven, or maybe even an eight!

I enter the asylum. (Okay, here we go. Drum roll, please…)

"Hello? Anybody home?"

No answer.

I follow a low droning sound and find them in the Sacred Television Temple sitting hypnotized in front of an old movie. It's *The Quiet Man.* The one filmed in Ireland with John Wayne. I know for a fact they have seen this one at least a dozen times. So the odds of some enthusiasm are in my favor. This time my presence will trump the Dim Blue Light.

With gusto I say, "Hello Mom. Hi Dad. Your boy is home!"

I wait for the excitement to kick in…

Silence.

Still waiting… nothing.

Okay, they're older. Let's give them a moment to warm up. Here we go…

Mom offers a quick, "Hi son."

Dad looks up, says nothing, and returns his trance-like gaze to the screen.

Still waiting… hang in there…I reach down to pet Max.

"Don't hurt him."

I'm not ready to run the white flag up the pole yet. "How are you two?"

Nothing.

"Can I get anybody anything?"

The breeze blows through the house. The TV drones on.

"Anyone care for a walk?"

Refusing to surrender I even throw in a song and dance routine straight out of *A Chorus Line*, but it's no contest. In a unanimous decision, the glowing box wins. I have officially entered a television dystopia. I take out my cell phone and call the starship *Enterprise*. "Beam me up Scotty!"

Well, the idea of coming out here looked good on paper.

Parental Pilgrimage Epiphanies

* Got to experience the feeling of invisibility.

* Saw myself clearly as the Patron Saint of Hopeless Causes.

* Now understand why the TV replaced me in the family Christmas photo.

Also. *The Quiet Man* reminded me of Ireland…

~~~~

Flashback:

Mom shocks me by accepting my invitation to travel with me in Ireland. There, we will celebrate my forty-second year by walking the hamlets of our ancestors. For the first time since childhood, just the two of us will spend an extended period of time together.

Upon arrival, the Emerald Isle blesses our adventure with a rare double rainbow. A sacred omen for sure.

That afternoon we stop at the Cliffs of Moher. These magnificent rocks rise seven hundred feet out of the Atlantic at Hags Head on Ireland's west coast. The day is unusually clear, allowing us to gaze across Galway Bay to the Aran Islands.

On our way to the high ground, Mom has trouble climbing a small hill. Her steps are shaky, and less assured. Of course, if any of this bothers her you would never know it, since she keeps any and all grievances securely to herself. Right before my eyes, my dear mother has suddenly grown old. My heart sinks as I realize father time has finally caught up with her.

One night by chance we end up at a small Bed & Breakfast rumored to be haunted. Never one to believe in such nonsense and despite dire warnings from the innkeepers, Mom scoffs at their stories of mischievous Leprechauns and a mysterious female Spirit called The Shee.

After a fitful night's sleep, we leave the haunted inn and travel to our next port of call. Upon arrival, she unpacks and discovers her slippers have vanished. "I know I put them right here in this compartment."

"How strange. Do you think it was a Spirit?"

She shakes her head. "I told you, I don't believe those things."

After we return from a walk on the beach, her slippers have mysteriously reappeared in the same compartment! My mother looks visibly shaken. "This is impossible. Do you think…maybe a spirit or something… no, it can't be… Besides, I don't believe in ghosts."

A few days later, we share our last dinner at an Oceanside bistro. A luminous full moon rises from the depths of the Irish Sea, enthralling us with its brilliance. When dessert arrives, I spontaneously sing 'Moon River' as we toast the moment, the trip, the country, and each other.

The following morning we sit in a small café once used by Oliver Cromwell as his headquarters and reminisce about our sacred sojourn.

"Thank you, my son, for your invitation and the trip of a lifetime. I will never forget this."

Suddenly the song 'Moon River' begins playing softly over the speakers. Startled, our eyes lock and she gasps, "Can you believe it?"

"No and yes. It's all so wonderful. Thank you, Mom."

"For what?"

"Mysterium Bellus et Fascinans—the beautiful and fascinating mystery, the unfathomable magic of this moment." I reach across the table and gently take her wrinkled hands.

"I love you, Mom."

"I love you too."

With tears in our eyes we look upon on each other with great affection.

The song plays on…

> *Two drifters, off to see the world,*
> *There's such a lot of world to see.*
> *We're after the same rainbow's end,*
> *Waiting 'round the bend,*
> *My huckleberry friend,*
> *Moon River and me.*

-23-

The Prisoner of the United States

Hitchhiker: What drove you to be successful?

Larry: I had to follow my dream. I couldn't continue working in a job I hated. So whatever it took to make it, obviously within the law, I was willing to do.

Hitchhiker: There's courage in that.

Larry: Not really, because I had no choice. I had to do this or I would die.

A few nights later I duck into a trendy Edgartown restaurant with some friends. The place is packed. We grab a table and begin soaking up the festive ambiance. While doing some restaurant reconnaissance, I notice a man with a familiar sheen to his head.

The Larry Phenomenon!

I have to go over. "Larry, my man!"

He greets me warmly and then announces to the group, "Hey everyone, this is *The Hitchhiker*!" His dinner party stirs with a palpable excitement. "He's the guy I've been telling you about!"

It's obvious they know about our mysterious encounters, and based on their response, I feel a little famous. "Larry, you're actually telling people about our nonsense?"

"Absolutely. It's too damn good not to!"

So is Larry telling his friends about *The Hitchhiker Phenomenon?*

Larry and I say goodbye and return to our respective universes.

The next day during another lunch on the porch at the Chilmark Store, a reporter from the Gazette randomly interviews me over the impending arrival of President Obama. (I secretly wonder if I am going to meet the President? Will he pick me up hitchhiking?) The paper is creating a special section about what Vineyarders, if given the chance, would say to Barack.

With his notebook in hand he asks, "So, what would you say to the President of the United States?"

"Need any help?"

"Seriously."

I take the pizza out of my mouth and respond. "Mr. President, I hope you have the courage to follow your convictions, and that history will smile on those who not only have a vision, but take bold action. I believe our society has reached a critical state where only a new paradigm of consciousness can transform and save us. What I would like to ask you, Mr. President, if I may borrow from Gandhi: What can I or any of us do to *BE* the change we wish to see in the world?"

When it's published the following week, I am disappointed to find the last few lines were edited out.

Three days later I'm riding my bike past the airport when a huge Marine helicopter passes directly overhead. Instinctively I know that's him, that's the President. My next thought is more practical. 'I hope I can get past security and up to the beach.'

Realizing a wayward vagabond on a bike is not much of a threat; the police decide to let me through. I peddle past people holding homemade signs with endearing slogans who hope to get a fleeting glimpse of their visiting king. A few miles beyond the airport, I realize that over the last few minutes not a single car has passed me in either direction.

His Highness must be coming. Someone sound the trumpets.

Sure enough, within seconds several state troopers on motorcycles fly past me. To avoid being squashed by the world's most elite motorcade, I begin peddling furiously. An officer pulls up next to me and shouts, "Get off the road! The President is coming!"

God, if I only had a nickel for every time I've heard that one!

Just in time, I turn onto a narrow patch of grass and park, as a magnificent display of temporal power passes within a few feet of my humble bicycle and me. Instinctively I hold up my arm and extend the peace symbol, offering a small blessing to the Imperial Motorcade. Isn't it interesting what difference a finger or two can make in terms of message?

In an instant the VIP Vortex passes, and calm returns to the scene. Though our lives pass within three feet of one another, our worlds could not be further apart. The birds sing on around me, apparently oblivious to the famous life form that has just flown by.

Imperial Impressions

* I feel like I just witnessed the transfer of a prisoner.

* It must be limiting to constantly see the world through bulletproof glass.

* I'm in my ninth week here, while the Prisoner of the United States only gets a meager seven-day furlough.

* The imperial Prisoner of the United States has a lot less freedom than meaningless old me.

This is instantly illustrated when I ride a hundred yards and stop, without a care in the world, at a small lemonade stand run by a coterie of young girls. Could the Prisoner of the United States do that without extensive planning? Or go nine weeks without wearing a coat or heaven forbid, a tie? Can he walk freely amongst the people or casually eat a slice of pizza on the porch at the Chilmark Store? Could he lie on the beach at night alone with his Creator, feeling at one with All That Is? Perhaps.

Most importantly, could he go hitchhiking and get picked up by Larry David?

I suddenly feel very fortunate and wonder why anyone would ever want to be the Prisoner of the United States.

-24-

The Greatest Show On Earth

Larry: Hey, wait a minute, you claim you have never seen my program. Right?

Hitchhiker: Yes, I have yet to see the greatest show on earth.

Larry: Well then, how did you know who I was?

Hitchhiker: I must have seen you on a Wheaties box.

It's the middle of August, and my house-sitting gig has come to an end. I look around for another place, but since it's the height of the season, nothing materializes. Maybe my magical run on the Vineyard is over. Hey, if I have to go, it's been a great ride. Instead of departing, I decide to tempt the fates and ask my parents if I can move back into the *Parental Asylum*.

I feel legitimately nervous as I make the two-mile sojourn out to my parent's habitat. Perhaps the old adage is true, 'You can't ever go home again.'

Mom is in the kitchen as I enter and pop the question. "Mom, can I come home?"

"Of course you can come back. I would love it, and even Dad said he missed having you around.

"Thank you Mom." I give her a hug and a kiss on the cheek.

"Can I make you an omelet?"

"Sure."

A portly Max comes up and nudges my mother's leg. "Oh look, the little man is letting me know he wants his breakfast."

"Mom I think you already fed him.

"Nonsense." She goes on. "Aren't we lucky to have each other? To share this time? We are so blessed. These days, I feel happy just sipping my coffee or working in the garden. When you think about the big picture, it is all so miraculous. God, every moment is precious. I love it."

I'm not exactly sure when it happened, but it's become apparent that my atheistic mother was abducted by aliens and then replaced with this deeply spiritual android. I would alert the proper authorities, but this replacement is so loving I don't have the heart.

Who is this person? The new Mom sounds more like a Himalayan monk, than the kidnapped woman who raised me. She doesn't seem to have a care in the world, only peace. How fortunate for her. Maybe we should all forget our unpleasant memories and live joyously. This form of ebullient amnesia would certainly help me.

"Mom, why are you always so welcoming?"

She looks out the window for a few moments, and I wonder if she forgot my question. But then she turns around, manages a slight smile, and sits down. "Well, when my older sister contracted polio, my mother had to make a choice. Only two of her three girls could stay, so I was sent away and raised by my Great-Grandmother."

"How old were you?"

"Ten. Part of me was relieved to get out of the house because my father was so cruel. He once knocked me out with his fist for wearing my hair a little differently."

"He hit you?"

"Right in the jaw. I was knocked out, and they took me to the hospital."

"Oh God. I am so sorry."

"It's okay. That was a long time ago."

"After you moved out, how often did you see your mother?"

"She was supposed to come visit every Sunday, but many times she never even showed up. I used to sit for hours in front of my granny's large picture window watching for her car." Mom shakes her head. "My clothes were freshly pressed, and I often held a few flowers from the garden in my hand. I would wait and wait…" Her voice trails off.

Sitting across from my mom, I imagine that sweet young girl alone with her pain and wonder if something inside her simply shut off. Feeling her heartache, I reach across the table and put my hand on top of hers. For a moment she gives me a loving look, the trace of a tear in the corner of her eye.

She looks off longingly into the distance…miles, or rather years away. "That's why it was so hard when my mother was dying. I felt like I was struggling to find someone I always wanted to know. But once again I was left alone at that window, waiting for a ghost that never showed up."

She turns back towards me and looks me in the eye. "That's why *you* are welcome. A child can always come home."

"Thank you Mom."

I move back home, and things are surprisingly harmonious. Believe it or not, I even manage to watch a little television with them. They seem to enjoy the courtroom shows, especially the one I call *Judge Yenta and The Trailer Park Court*. Each episode consists of participants apparently immune from humiliation, who stand in front of the well lit Yenta arguing about life and death issues such as: he stole my cigarettes, she pawned my bong, they never paid back the bail money, she lost the remote, etc. Though I find the show fascinating, it's not nearly as entertaining as my parent's running commentary.

"She should have never let that bum move into the trailer. Not with that haircut and all those tattoos. He looks like trouble. Get a job, loser!"

Sensing an opportunity for some solidarity, I jump in. "Why does she have curlers in her hair? Where could she possibly be going later that is more important than being on national television right now?"

"Maybe she has a date," Mom suggests. "Stick around. This is a special one-hour episode."

Researchers say that the average person watches nine years of television in their lifetime, but I sometimes think my parents have decided to watch their combined eighteen years in one sitting.

"No thanks. I'm going to ride my bike up island and take a swim."

Amidst all this electronic jurisprudence, Max has been giving himself a head to toe cleaning. Max is a huge believer in the healing power of licking, though with what's he doing in this moment, he runs the risk of being arrested by the vice squad. I reach down to pet Max.

"Don't hurt him."

On my way to the beach I drop into the Edgartown Stop & Shop, pick up a sandwich and step into the checkout line to pay. The bagger asks, "Paper or plastic?"

"No thank you. I don't need a bag."

She smiles. "Do you remember me?"

I give her a closer look and say, "It took me a moment because the little hat threw me, but I have to admit, the brown polyester really works for you." Homeless Lady laughs and playfully slaps my arm. I look down at her nametag. "So it's Linda. How nice to finally put a name to your face."

"I'm doing much better and even found a place to live."

Happily removing the word 'homeless' from her title, I say, "Congratulations Linda."

"Oh, and I've decided to stay on the Island through the winter." She gestures towards the store and adds, "They really need me here."

"We all do. Thanks for giving me hope."

"I gave *you* hope?" She tilts her head. "How?"

"When things improve for one of us, they improve for all of us. The whole world is a little better today because *you* are, and this gives me hope. There are no small acts."

"Ah, there you go again, talkin' all crazy."

"I told you I tend to ramble. Look, everyday billions of things go right: people helping each other, random acts of kindness, bridges that work, flights that arrive, and yet none of it makes the news. All of these small acts make the world go around."

"Maybe you should be a preacher?"

"Am I that bad? I could use a job. Being a professional bodysurfer doesn't pay like it used to. Maybe I should fill out an application?"

She smiles again. "Get out of here."

"Take care of yourself, Linda."

As I turn to leave, she gently touches my arm. "I owe you this." She is holding a twenty-dollar bill.

"I knew you were good for it. But do me a favor." I place my hands around her hand with the money. "Find someone who needs it more than us and invest in them. It's your turn to pay it forward."

She looks down at our hands and then up at me. "I will."

For a moment our eyes meet and I know. I don't understand what I know, but I know.

"Goodbye Linda."

I take my lunch over to a bench in the park and think about Linda. How far does a person have to fall in their life for a job paying minimum wage to become a high point? Some children wander past me, their faces reflecting the joy of a bright summer day. Do any of them currently dream of someday becoming a store clerk? Or sitting behind a desk for hours on end concerned with menial things?

What happens to a person who no longer has dreams?

A disheveled old man who looks like a drifter wanders up and sits down next to me. I casually extend my hand with half of the sandwich.

He takes it without missing a beat. "Thanks, friend."

We sit in silence, eating our daily bread as we watch the people pass by.

Out of the blue he says, "This is truly the greatest show on Earth." He turns and winks at me. "Don't you think?"

"WHAT?" I stammer.

"This is truly the greatest show on Earth." The Magical Mystery Man repeats, winking again.

How did my observation from the other evening come back to me verbatim?

"But is the show real?" he asks.

"It appears to be."

"Maybe it's a dream…"

"You mean like Plato's Allegory of the Cave, where people mistake the flickering shadows on the wall for reality?"

"Yes." The Magical Mystery Man says, "Sort of like smoke rings in our mind. Perhaps we come here to learn and experience love."

"I like that." I am enjoying this enlightened old vagrant. I finish my sandwich and get on my bike. "Thanks for the conversation. You taught me a lot."

"Nothing you didn't already know and haven't thought for yourself. You were generous to share your lunch with me. It's good for a man to live magnanimously. Who knows, maybe I'll see you around."

"I hope so."

"Oh, one last thing," he adds. "Mind if I throw some Shakespeare at you."

"Go ahead."

"Do you remember Polonius's last piece of advice to his son Laertes?"

"Can't say I do."

"To thine own self be true."

"That's a good one to live by."

Still hungry after sharing my lunch, I head towards Chilmark for my daily slice of pizza. (With so much eating taking place, maybe this book belongs in the food section.) I grab a heavenly piece of pie and settle into a rocking chair. Three tiny sparrows gather around my feet for any crumb I may be willing to part with. In between bites, I tear off bits of crust and scatter them for my winged friends.

This must be my day to feed the masses.

A trio of boys around the age of ten cautiously make their way over to me. I break the ice by asking, "How are you guys?" That's all the prompting they need, and they're off to the races. They proceed to give me their entire summer rundown in intricate detail.

Ten is such a wonderful age. These three are not concerned with the housing market or the politics down at the office. There's no stress over the state of their marriage. Life still looks magical and full of infinite possibilities. Their world is overflowing with mysteries to be uncovered and explored.

Here on the porch they seem delighted to have (what appears to be) an adult giving them the time, respect and attention they deserve. Later, in a moment of ultimate bonding, I confide to them my secret: though I may look older, on the inside I'm also ten years old.

"Just like Josh in the movie *Big*?" They ask.

"Exactly."

Eventually the sparrows and the boys depart.

I walk down to the beach past a group of teenagers typing away on their hand held devices, while a few feet away one of the most gorgeous panoramic views imaginable invites adoration. When did we get so obsessed with these tiny screens?

I gaze out at the water and wonder, how did I ever get so lucky? A moment later, four lifeguards sprint past me towards a small crowd gathering along the shore. I watch as someone is pulled from the sea. I remember my own experience and hope this person shares a similar outcome. When one of the lifeguards returns I ask, "Is he going to be okay?"

"No, he didn't make it."

And just like that, another life comes to an end. A man dying seems oddly out of place on such a spectacular day. The sun is shining brilliantly and the ocean appears to be no different, yet the world has definitely changed. There is nothing like birth, death and disaster to bring our priorities into alignment.

Who was this man? Does he have a family? When he woke up this morning, did this day seem any different? Did he have any plans for this evening? He came to the beach, went for a swim, and never made it out of the water.

I am reminded, once again, that all things must pass. Everything, everyone, all things will one day no longer be. We move like a shooting star through the ether of time. As an organism we have the capacity to hold this truth, and for some this awareness is crippling, while for others liberating. For me it makes the collective's wanton obsession with material things an interesting choice.

I leave the beach and begin my ride back towards Edgartown. Along the way I listen to the song of my own inner stillness. Even with its tragedy, 'life is still the greatest show on Earth.'

From a bench across the street, a loud voice is answering my thought, "YES! YES!"

Is it possible? No, it can't be. What's *HE* doing way up here? It's my lunch date from way back in Edgartown, the Magical Mystery Man! I'm so shocked I almost ride straight into a tree. How did he get so far so fast?

The Magical Mystery Man waves again and yells, "YES! YES!"

Now I'm convinced he's not of this world and then I have a peculiar thought, "Maybe this is how Larry feels every time I somehow appear out of nowhere?" Is this simply *The Larry Phenomenon* gone rogue?

When I return home my dad reminds me something like this has happened once before...

~~~~

Flashback:

Dad, Mom, and I are having lunch at the Farm Neck Country Club. Dad points to a man who is sitting alone across the room. "I see that guy all over the Island: the Edgartown Post Office, the hardware store in Vineyard Haven, the library, everywhere...I feel like we know each other, but for the life of me I can't place him."

"You two kind of look alike," I say. "Maybe he's your guardian angel?"

Dad shakes his head. "I don't believe in that stuff."

"Have you ever spoken to one another?"

"Not that I can recall. He just seems familiar. Strange, he always has the same clothes on and he usually nods or smiles at me. Maybe I know him from my old neighborhood back in Brooklyn."

I survey the layout of the room and say, "Well, he has to pass our table when he leaves. Why don't you say hello?"

"I think I will."

The man across the room puts his leftovers in a white box, glances over at Dad and smiles, then heads our way. But just before reaching us, he turns and goes into the bathroom. At least thirty minutes pass by, and he still hasn't come out.

Dad asks, "Do you think he's okay? He's been in there a long time."

"He must have really had to go," I joke.

Mom chimes in, "Oh for heaven's sake."

"I'm sorry. Seriously, let's go check on him,"

Dad and I enter the restroom and find it empty.

"What the hell?" Dad says. "Wait, look!" There on the counter is his white to-go box.

"Dad, where did he go? There is no other exit and no windows. How could he vanish?"

We never got any answers, and my Dad never saw him again.

~~~~~

25

Dancing With The Cosmos

Hitchhiker: Larry, do you believe in a Higher Power or Universal Intelligence?

Larry: Oh God, yes! I mean you have to believe in something higher and wiser. Especially when you look at all of this…

(Makes a sweeping gesture towards heavens)

Hitchhiker: It is so miraculous.

Larry: And how perfect it is.

(He shakes his head.)

I'm not sure what IT is, but there is DEFINITELY something.

Opening the door I hear music playing and see two champagne glasses sitting by the fireplace. After checking around downstairs I walk up to the master bedroom. I enter the room to find the Miracle locked in a sultry embrace with another man. Confronted by my presence, the two of them start laughing and…

I awaken to see the asylum's familiar walls.

Though I never left the safety of my bedroom, I feel destroyed, heartbroken, and in a terrible state of panic. It takes a while, but my heart and I finally calm down and stop hurting.

Sitting at my parent's kitchen table nursing a stiff cup of tea, I begin to wonder. How is the suffering in my nightmare any different from the pain I feel while awake? The dream only hurt because I believed it to be real. What if I woke up in my daily life and saw all my suffering as an illusion?

~~~~

Flashback:

My longtime Nashville mentor Nelson Andrews is dying. His son calls to say, "Dad is not going to make it through the night and wants to say goodbye to you and the Miracle."

Nelson, always a big fan of the Miracle, does not know of our dissolution. With his health failing, I didn't have the heart to tell him.

Having not spoken to the Miracle lately, I am hesitant to contact her. The last couple of times we interacted were deeply painful, and I am in no hurry to feel that way again. Still, I feel it would be selfish to deprive Nelson of a final goodbye, so I relent and call.

We meet outside his home. "How are you, Miracle?"

"I am so sad about Nelson."

"Me too. He's been like a father to me. He's not even gone, and I already miss him."

His loving family is gathered around him, and I feel honored to be included in his inner circle. I recall our countless lunches, the constant support, phone calls that opened doors, and how this pillar of the community took 'nobody me' under his wing. Mostly, I remember the things he modeled: a healthy family life, balance, service, and humility. Nelson taught not by telling, but by living.

Now here at the end, I bow down in front of this iconic figure. We hold hands and look deeply into each other's eyes. "Nelson, thank you for everything. For all of the kindness, and for all of the wisdom."

With tubes running from his failing body, he musters the strength for a few wise words. "It was all stupidity, my friend." He is humble to the end. "I want to tell you something important." He points towards the Miracle, sitting by my side with tears in her eyes. "You need to hang on to her. You two have something special. Never let her go. Don't ever lose each other."

His words are like daggers in my chest. I drop my head and gently weep. After a few moments I pull myself together and offer comfort to his longtime wife, the ever loyal and ever loving Sue.

She tears up and shakes her head. "Even after all these years, it never feels like enough time. You are always left wanting one more day."

I take Nelson's hands once last time, "Goodbye, my friend. You will be missed, though I'm sure I will see you again." I put my arms around his frail shoulders and try to seal his Presence within me.

After a while the Miracle and I depart.   We silently embrace one last time, before reluctantly returning to the emptiness of our separate lives.

~~~~

Lying there in the dark pondering all this, I remember an interesting story. Last spring my friend and I stood in his yard wondering why a huge walnut tree was dying. This seemed strange since all of the other trees were in perfect health.   He recalled standing next to the same tree a year earlier and saying to his wife, "When we build the swimming pool, we'll have to cut this walnut tree down."

If it's true we create our experience, this story demonstrates what the quantum physicists call 'The Observer Effect.' This is where the observed phenomenon is influenced by what the observer expects.   This fact has been proven scientifically, though I don't need to see the lab sheets to believe it.

I am living it.

I come to the painful conclusion that my relationship with the Miracle is the dead walnut tree in my neglected garden. Despite her loving efforts, I continually pushed her away. Because I did not believe in her or us, our relationship came to a slow and painful death. Just like the walnut tree. It's time for me to own this difficult truth.   With this realization comes the possibility for change and a ray of hope for a new tomorrow.

Pondering this epiphany, I peacefully fall back asleep.

When I awaken, it's as if a heavy weight has been lifted from my heart. I feel a sense of peace and no longer carry a negative charge around my feelings for the Miracle.

That evening, I'm back on my favorite Water Street bench enjoying an ice cream cone and listening to Troubadour Dave caress the night air with his unique muse. The old minstrel is in rare form as he launches into Bob Dylan's *Mr. Tambourine Man*. The Japanese believe in *Kotodama*, that mystical powers dwell in words and names. I experience this viscerally as the lyrics, and I merge into one life form.

> *Take me disappearin'*
> *Through the smoke rings of my mind*
> *Down the foggy ruins of time*
> *Far past the frozen leaves,*
> *The haunted, frightened trees*
> *Out to the windy beach*
> *Far from the twisted reach of crazy sorrow*
> *Yes, to dance beneath the diamond sky*
> *With one hand waving free*
> *Silhouetted by the sea*
> *Circled by the circus sands*
> *With all memory and fate*
> *Driven deep beneath the waves*
> *Let me forget about today until tomorrow...*

I stagger away and unconsciously begin to wander around the back streets of Edgartown. I suddenly awaken in front of a small old cottage. Wait a minute. I know this place...

~~~~~

Flashback:

The twenty-year old me plays the piano for a tiny woman named Mrs. Wuerth. In her late nineties, she has shrunken down to the size of one of those porcelain lawn jockeys. Fortunately for me the size of her spirit stands in direct contrast to the diminutive form she is in the process of shedding.

The two of us talk for hours and no matter what the subject, she enthusiastically exclaims, "Isn't it WONDERFUL?"

My flawed piano playing, the latest crush, the crushing blow, the bees pollinating her flowers, my presence, our friendship, the endless mysteries, the noble quest, impending death, the smell of babies…And she always rejoices, "Isn't it WONDERFUL?"

I am much too young to know it, but the tiny little elf is right.

"It is WONDERFUL!"

Including the fact that Mrs. Wuerth, pronounced 'worth,' is so perfectly named. She didn't know the price of anything, but Mrs. Wuerth knew the value of everything.

The next summer I arrive and immediately ride my bike to her home. I come looking for reunion, but instead discover an empty house. Sometime during the winter Mrs. Wuerth passed away. My tiny friend with the huge heart is gone.

"Isn't it WONDERFUL?"

Yes…but just a little less so than before.

~~~~~

Tonight I am seeing her spirit in all things wonderful.

I think about the words of Wordsworth in *Imitations of Immortality*. "Our birth is but a sleep of forgetting. Not in entire forgetfulness, and not in utter nakedness, but trailing clouds of glory do we come from God, who is our home. Heaven lies about us in our infancy!"

I walk down to the lighthouse and sit on the beach near the water. Looking up at the heavens I ask, "Must we always lose the ones we love?"

A shooting star crosses the horizon, and I think about Mrs. Wuerth, the Miracle, Nelson and my father…

~~~~~

Flashback:

Dad's sister Claire has terminal cancer and is in a long, slow decline. She desperately wants to see her closest sibling one last time. Dad promises to come to New Jersey, but keeps putting it off. He just can't bring himself to face the buried skeletons of their past: the childhood deprivation, the absentee father, the collective suffering—it is simply too much.

He talks of seeing Claire, but one sad day it is too late, and she is gone. There is no goodbye, no closure, and no peace. Only grief.

Around this time Dad's mother is hospitalized for depression. She has been kept in the dark about her daughter's condition. The day after his sister dies, my father drives over to visit his mom. She surprises him by inquiring about Claire, feeling as if something is very wrong. He assures her that everything is fine, kisses her on the cheek, and promises to come visit tomorrow.

That night in her sleep, his mother dies.

After the funerals, my father discovers his remaining sister has stolen the inheritance intended for each of the grandchildren. When confronted, she offers to split the money with Dad, but deprive the daughters who have recently buried their mother. Since this proposal is unacceptable, he implores his last surviving relative to do the right thing. She refuses, and my dad never speaks to her again.

In the span of a week, my dad loses his entire family.

I see a man frozen in shock who moves through the world like a zombie. When I ask him if he is okay, he stares back blankly and simply says, "yes."

In the days that follow Dad begins to shut down and withdraw from the world. At sixteen, I have no clue how to reach him. The decline is subtle and slow, like watching a ship sail farther and farther away, until a time comes when only the memory of the magnificent vessel remains.

~~~~~

So maybe that is what happened. How did I miss it? My father's tragic predicament must have gotten lost in the limitations of my teenage egocentrism.

Something in me shifts, and I see a man with faults, fears, disappointments and pain. Just like me.

With this realization, comes an overwhelming sense of compassion and love. My heart aches in solitude yet I am surrounded by Grace.

The sky invites me to the water's edge to write the names of those who have hurt me in the sand.

A small act.

With my knees on the beach, I take my time and begin to sketch…my parents, the Miracle, the world, and most importantly, myself.

The night speaks…

"Let the sacred sea wash the slate clean, and all that is held…shall forever be released."

My eyes well up, and the water begins to run down my cheeks. Tiny drops fall one by one into the ancient sand. These are the tears of forgiveness.

A gentle wave cascades over my grievances, returning the shoreline to its pristine condition. The next wave washes over and emancipates me. And then another…

Once again, through the Sacred waters of the Vineyard, I am reborn.

My ego longs to cling to its lofty lonely perch, piously screeching the mantra, "Your sins are greater than mine." Yet a loving Master once whispered, "Let he who is without sin cast the first stone."

I wish to cast no more stones.

Looking back over the summer and all the people who crossed my path, I find a common thread; we are all hopelessly human, simply doing the best we can with what little we have. My father, Broken-Hearted Bill, The White Hairs, The Bluebloods, the famous, the homeless, Troubadour Dave, and Dealmaker Doug. In the end, we all just want to belong and be loved.

"Love them and let them be as they may."

Yes.

For a long time I lay on my back in the sand, in awe of my celestial neighborhood. I hear whispers and echoes on the breeze and remember Ralph Waldo Emerson once asked, "What if the stars only came out once every thousand years?" I ponder this as another shooting star passes through the night sky.

Paul Hawken recently said of Emerson's quote, "What would we do to celebrate such a rare, magnificent occurrence? Would new religions spring up around this miraculous happening? Perhaps. But instead, the stars come out every night while we stay inside watching television."

The Cosmos continues to dance with my spirit, and what is left of me begins to merge with that which cannot possibly be named. The wind blows through me as if I am transparent, a fleeting hologram briefly dancing in time. The

Great Mystery of Being lovingly shares a few insights with its humble creation...

The true and eternal You is greater than what can ever be imagined or known.

The cage you unconsciously construct with your limitations is always open and you are free to run from its claustrophobic confines singing and dancing.

Everything—the pain, suffering, insanity, mistakes, and disasters—work in perfection and are guided by Infinite Love and Intelligence.

What appears as chaos is manifested consciousness so complex it is beyond your level of comprehension.

Whatever unfolds is completely Self-originated and here to help you transcend your current level of comprehension towards a greater awareness and understanding of Self.

There is much to know yet nothing new to learn.

True freedom comes not in finding the answers, but from joyfully living with the questions.

Trust the Divine Process and you shall find peace.

I lie there for a while, allowing this to permeate my cells. My dance with the cosmos has taken me to places that words cannot follow.

Once again, touched by magic, I am never the same.

26

Resonance & Reunion

Hitchhiker: Larry, what matters most?

Larry: That is a really big question.

(Thinking for a long time.)

Being true to yourself and doing whatever it is that you really have to do.

I'm talking about the thing you love to do…

In your one and only life…

You have to do that.

It's early the next morning, and I am listening to the sound of the phone ringing in my ear. 'Miracle, please pick up. Ring, ring, ring…pick it up…this feels too important to leave a message.'

"Hello?"

"Good morning. It's me."

"It's early. Are you okay?"

"I had to hear your voice." I share what I can of last night's experience under the stars then add, "I wish you could be here and feel the magic of this place. It is truly sacred."

"Me too. Do you remember back in Del Mar when we talked about you showing me around the Vineyard?"

"Yes, of course." I begin to open my heart. "Miracle, I don't feel like we've been apart this summer, because in a way you are always with me. You live just beneath the surface of every moment as a silent witness to all that I am. I've got to be honest it haunts me that I never gave us all of me. I keep asking myself, what would have happened if I had put us first and loved you in an unguarded way?"

She begins to softly cry.

"I'm sorry, sweet Miracle. I'm so very sorry."

"Me too. I miss you. I always miss you."

I realize the time has come for me to cross the room, heart in hand, and once again ask her to dance. "Why don't you come to the Vineyard? Perhaps an Island reunion would be healing."

There is a long pause on the other end of the phone.

Will she step in my direction? Or once and for all, are we truly over? Does she have it in her heart to give me another chance? Or is it simply too late? I feel vulnerable in the silence. There is so much at stake here.

I hear her breathing on the line.

I go for broke. "There's a line in *The Prophet,* 'The depth and connection of love is never truly known until the moment it is lost.' I feel that way with us. I've been there, lived there, and mourned there. Don't make me go back there."

"Oh my love."

"Do you remember that Rumi quote we loved? 'Out beyond ideas of right-doing and wrongdoing, there is a field—I will meet you there.' I believe that field is on this island. Meet me there."

"I will meet you there."

I cannot put my elation into words. It's as if some higher authority has granted me a pardon. Like every life, mine has circumstances I wish had turned out differently. Lovers often pray for a second chance to go back and make wrong things right. This time the prayer was answered.

For our reunion to occur, a few practical things have to fall into place. Where will we stay? The *Parental Asylum* is not an option. After all, hasn't she suffered enough? I make some calls and check the real estate listings, but completely strike out. Since it's the end of August and the peak of the season, there's nothing to be found. I reluctantly let it go and hand it over to the gods of reunification.

That night at the Atlantic Restaurant, I am attempting to explain *The Larry Phenomenon* to the Great Mongolian Donut Sage. "It's really strange, but the whole thing feels like an episode of the Twilight Zone." A moment later as if on cue, Larry enters, grabs a drink at the bar, spots me, and heads my way.

In a low-key way that implies it's no big deal, I say, "Hi Larry."

In shock the Sage turns to Larry and says, "He was just talking about you."

"That's what we do," Larry says casually.

"How do you say *The Larry Phenomenon* in Mongolian?"

"What?" The Sage asks.

"Never mind…"

"Things are kind of strange between us," Larry adds. It's like an episode of the Twilight Zone!"

"HE JUST SAID THAT TOO!" The Sage practically screams. "THIS IS TRULY WEIRD!"

Larry and I just shrug. Then, in acknowledgement of our mysterious dynamic, we shake hands.

Though I'm enjoying our reunion I add, "Larry, you realize if you keep this up, I'm going to have to get a restraining order."

Larry cracks up. After a few minutes the annoying herd begins to run him off. The flock starts demanding a picture, a handshake, an autograph, and his attention, which though intrusive, he handles gracefully.

Larry scans the scene one last time and says, "I better get going." He begins to leave, but turns back towards me with a mischievous look in his eye. "By the way, have you kept your promise and seen any of my stuff?"

Ohhhhhhh…

And that's when it happened… *The Hitchhiker Lean-Back!*

I quickly recover by employing *The Summer Weather Defense*. "Larry, come on, it's the summer and the weather's been perfect! I know YOU are not a nature guy, but I can't stay inside a dark room and watch endless hours of television when the sun is shining. Even for your unparalleled comedic genius."

His arms are crossed and he's smiling, but the jury's still out.

I continue to plead my case. "Trust me Larry, once I get home, or heaven forbid, the weather goes in the tank, I'll watch your show. You held up your end of the bargain, and I'll honor mine."

The verdict is in. He points a playful finger at me and says, "Okay. But remember, you promised."

We shake hands warmly, and parting the mortal masses like Moses in his mighty wake, Larry vanishes into the evening mist.

God bless *The Larry Phenomenon!*

As I'm leaving the restaurant, I run into the Lovebirds Emily and Sam who invite me to go sailing in the morning.

The next day I arrive at the dock, coffee in hand, take in the fresh morning air, and scan the horizon for the Lovebirds. "There they are!"

My cell phone rings and it's the Miracle. "I have some bad news and some good news. I just got a wonderful new job offer."

"You did? Wow. But what's the good news?"

"Very funny. But here's the bad part: the latest I can begin is a week from tomorrow."

"Oh." I feel my stomach tighten as the prospects for our reunion suddenly look bleak.

"So if I'm coming to the Vineyard, it has to happen this week. Have you had any luck finding a place?"

"Not yet. August is the height of the season, and the Island is packed."

"Well, they want my answer on the job by 5:00. I'm sorry. I so wanted to come."

So much for our romantic reunion. I am devastated.

I board the USS Lovebird, and we set sail for the open sea. Before we are even out of the Harbor, Emily asks, "Is your Miracle coming to the Vineyard?"

"I'm working on it, but I need to find a place for us to stay."

"Really? We're staying at Sam's family home in town, and the house is huge. You two are welcome to use the entire upstairs for as long as you want."

I immediately dial the Miracle and break out the great news like a bottle of Dom Perignon. Excited, she shifts into high gear and begins packing for her pilgrimage north.

After a sleepless night, I am down at the ferry dock nervously awaiting her arrival. Since I have no idea how we will relate or what kind of chemistry we'll create, I try to approach her visit without expectations. I do know that no matter what happens, if we are tender and careful with each other, a lot of healing will take place.

As she steps off the boat, my heart leaps from my chest. I had forgotten how strikingly beautiful she is. We hug, and the power of our love floods over me. Her skin feels warm, and her hair so soft against my face. Her heart is pounding, no wait, it's mine. In many ways, this is our first embrace. The feelings arrive in huge waves as I am immersed in the depth of our connection. I realize now, this bond has always been there.

With tears in our eyes, we finally let go.

"Miracle, I never thought we would have this chance again. Holding you still feels like coming home."

"I had forgotten what you feel like, what US feels like."

"Until this moment I had no idea how much I missed you."

"God, I am so glad I'm here."

"Me too."

Not all of our interactions are filled with smiles and laughter. There are also painful and raw talks. Anger and indignation arise spiked with "How could you ever do that to me?" moments. We also listen, hear, affirm, own, apologize, and seek forgiveness. Which over the days and through healing tears, is eventually given.

This is our own Vineyard Truth & Reconciliation Council, and though at times extremely challenging, we navigate through these discordant rapids to a harmonious place of resonance and reunion.

I recall the wise words shared with me throughout this summer and begin to integrate and inure them into our courtship. In my old selfish days it was all about me, and what I wanted. Now, I consciously put the Miracle first. After all, why are her desires and dreams any less important than mine? I try to listen more and say less. (With mixed results. Okay, okay…this still needs a lot of work.)

Though we obviously share a deep and rich history, the relationship suddenly feels brand new. May the old 'Us' rest in peace. Something fresh and beautiful is being created. This nascent energy does not merely work it thrives.

The magic of the Island softens us and provides a space in which to grow. We start each morning meandering through the backstreets of Edgartown down to the Harborview Hotel for coffee and conversation. Sitting on the porch, we hold hands and watch the boats sail out to sea.

"This whole Island feels like the sound of children's laughter," she says. I must say The Miracle has always had a unique way of putting things.

"So then New York City would feel like the sound of children whining?" She smiles and gives me a playful pat on the arm.

The afternoons are spent hanging out at the beach in Aquinnah, taking long walks past multi-colored cliffs hundreds of feet high. The cliffs, etched over time by six glaciers, remain a sacred place for the Island's original inhabitants, the Wampanog Indian Tribe. We take the moist clay and cover ourselves from head to toe. The sun dries the adobe earth creating a full body mask and removing the toxins from our skin and hearts. Encased in clay, we swim in a deserted cove as the water washes our souls clean.

This hallowed native ground blesses and heals us.

As the sun drifts into the sea, I realize I have finally found someone who will watch the sunset with me. With an old wool blanket wrapped around us, we watch the afterglow fill the sky. We sit with our mouths agape at the brilliance of the changing colors. "I can see why you love the Vineyard," she says.

"This place has always felt like home to me. Like you, it is beautiful and magical."

"Ah...I'm so grateful to be here." She puts her hand on top of mine. "Thank you."

"I finally understand the value of commitment. Love is a lot like nuclear power. If it's not protected in a safe container, it can be extremely harmful and dangerous." I hold my hands out to create one half of a box. "Now put your hands with mine."

She does so forming a perfect square.

"You see, Miracle? That space is the metaphorical vessel in which we exist. If either of us is only half in," I say, taking away one of my hands, "it will create a hole. Then everything we put into us would eventually leak out."

"You're right." She says, dropping her hands into the sand.

"Love may be precious and healing but it is also extremely powerful. So we always need to safeguard our relationship consciously."

She puts her hands back up. "I'm in."

I do the same. "Me too."

The evenings are spent overlooking the Edgartown Harbor at the Atlantic Restaurant where the wonderful Maitre d' Jaime treats us like royalty; our favorite wine is waiting on the table, the latest creation from the kitchen to be sampled, and a rich desert completes the culinary love fest.

These dinners feel like the coronation of my summer.

In the midst of all this romance and felicity, I often pause to appreciate the magnificent soul beside me. So many times this summer the possibility of our reconnection seemed utterly impossible. Yet here we are holding hands, falling in love again.

The Swiss writer Alain de Botton once said, "We should not feel embarrassed by our difficulties, only by our failure to grow anything beautiful from them."

I feel grateful to be given the opportunity to right old wrongs and to love at last more unconditionally.

"Miracle, would you be willing to move back in with me? I want to give us another try."

She hugs me, kisses my cheek and says, "YES!"

We decide this thing called "Us" can be rebuilt from the ruins of the past, and the two of us can learn from our mistakes, grow stronger, and move forward as one. Together we venture forth on newborn legs, one tentative and tender step at a time.

In the end, I learn that love and love alone is…what matters most.

27

The End of the Ride

(Larry pulls the car over and stops.)

Hitchhiker: I still think we should go to lunch.

Larry: (Laughing) Absolutely not. Now get out of here. Who knows, I'll probably see you around. (Larry the prophet?)

Hitchhiker: I hope so. Thank you. I really enjoyed the ride.

Larry: Me too. Now get out.

My original two-week stay has now stretched into its eleventh week, and there is no denying the first smell of fall on the breeze. Autumn always turns me inward, making me nostalgic for the warm, carefree days of summer.

With the hope of celebrating my dad's eighty-fifth birthday, I once again extend my stay. A lavish dinner is planned, but Dad begs off with a stomachache. The celebration is postponed twice and then cancelled. On Dad's BIG day, the Miracle and I stop by. We discover him in front of, where else, the Dim Blue Light. I try to get his attention to wish him well, but Dad only says, "Can you move aside. You're blocking the screen."

How fitting. I humbly acquiesce and depart...

~~~~~

Flashback:

My father and I sit across from one another, each devouring a huge bowl of ice cream. I am twelve years old. The only sound in the room is our spoons hitting the dish.

I look up, and our eyes gently come together. Usually my dad looks away when this happens. But not this time. His face is open and unguarded, and for some strange reason, I don't see my father looking back at me. Instead I behold a child with soft brown eyes, longing to be loved.

We continue to gaze at each other, and I am overwhelmed with unconditional love. I have never looked upon another in this way, let alone my father.

We pause in silence.

For a timeless moment, the soul of my father allows me to look upon it and feel the radiance of its Being.

Though my dad has always been close by, never until this moment have I truly seen him.

~~~~~

On the way back I realize that, while I long to connect with him on a deeper level, for now I must settle on proximity. Dad's struggle with intimacy does not signify a lack of caring. We love each other deeply, but are unable to share time in the landscape of the other's preferences.

I tried to sit with him in the Sacred Television Temple and watch the news. Or as I like to call it, "What Went Wrong Today," but the endlessly-talking-well-coifed-heads drive me crazy. I look to find a shred of truth among the carnival barkers, but any sustained viewing leaves me intellectually emaciated. Why would he spend his precious time focused on all the insanity in the world and television's constant message of fear and consumption?

When I ask Dad to watch the sunset, he declines. Dad is not comfortable sitting with me on the beach, and I can't watch *Seinfeld* reruns. We are two peas in a pod. It's that rare kind of stalemate where both of the players lose.

Even when the Universe personally sent its creator, Larry David (of *Seinfeld*—not life), my ignorance prevented me from hearing the *Gospel of Seinfeld*. When Larry chastised me for not watching his program and asked the rhetorical question, 'How can you deny yourself so much pleasure?' I still didn't get it.

I mistakenly thought that our mutual high ground sat somewhere else when in reality it is everywhere. Now I see the message of *The Gospel of Seinfeld:* how can I deny myself the priceless pleasure of sitting with my father, the man who gave up so much for me, whom I love so dearly, under ANY circumstances?

Yes. How could I ever say no?

Someday, as sure as the sunset I so adore, I will no longer have that opportunity. Over the past thirty years I have repeatedly tried to connect with my father. Most of the time I have found the door closed. Yet every once in a while we share a moment so pure, it is well worth the years of rejection and pain. While there is life, there is hope, so I must always keep trying.

In the blink of an eye, my final days on the Island drift by.

On my last Vineyard morning, I take the Miracle to the airport and place my house key in her hand, comforted by the thought that she'll be there to hold me tonight.

Filled with love, I return to the asylum. I grab my bike and take one long last ride beside the ocean. For a moment I ponder the mystery of *The Larry Phenomenon*. What was that all about? Maybe this is only the beginning and the phenomenon is open-ended? Though I hope my next book doesn't turn out to be *Camping With Larry David*.

Laughing, I scream to the wind, "Larry, where the hell are you? It's time for us to say goodbye!"

Perhaps there is no farewell.

I stop along the beach and give thanks for the many summer miles I have traveled, both on land and in spirit.

Back at that asylum Dad is withdrawn and decides not to take the trip with us to the airport. I have failed to reach him this summer, at least on his terms, and this saddens me. We hug and I tell him I love him. He stands in the doorway as I step outside. Turning around, I put my hand on his chest, look deep into his world-weary eyes and say, "Please take care of yourself, and know that I love you very much."

I back away and he lets the screen door slowly close between us. For a moment he stands there looking at me. What is he thinking? Gazing at each other, I lift my hand and place it on the screen.

Time passes…

He slowly lifts his hand and sets it softly against mine. Our fingers press together, man and boy, teacher and student, father and son. Now, with only a thin screen between us, we touch at last.

Détente.

"Goodbye Dad."

On the ride to the airport, Mom and I hold hands. I share many well-deserved yet inadequate platitudes. I offer them freely and lovingly, knowing they may well be forgotten before she returns home. Though on some level, they will never be lost. In times like these, words are such hopelessly inadequate creatures. Yet they are all we mortals have to bridge the imaginary gaps between us.

How do I ever thank her for the gift of life? For demanding the best, yet accepting the worst. For everything she did. "Mom, do you ever wonder, when you say goodbye to someone, if it will be the last time you see them?"

"I hope you're not worried about me, Son, because I plan to be here for a very long time. Besides, I can't leave you now," she says, ever the mother, soother, and rock. "We have so much more to share."

But now I see my rock is so much older, and time has worn down her pseudo veneer to expose something quite luxurious.

When the boarding call comes, I hold on tight and thank her again. Our eyes meet, and I burst into uncontrollable tears. I cry like a baby for all the pain endured by her, my dad, and me. I weep for that which will never be understood and for the unfathomable love that exists between us.

"Goodbye Mom."

"Goodbye Son."

I stagger away awash in the glory of pure emotion and the pain of primal separation and stand on the tarmac in the thick mist.

Where is Humphrey Bogart when I need him?

Before I know it, we are off the ground, and I am in the air. My heart overflowing, I look back through tears as my magical summer fades from view.

Now I know the Universe *can* be trusted to lift me up.

I must say yes, I must always say yes. For with love, all things are possible.

The Ancient Gods of Love were right. *You never know when magic might happen.*

Sometimes we have to dance between the raindrops.

The clouds part, and the bright golden sun appears on the horizon.

I lift my arm slightly, smile, and stick out my thumb. Perhaps this could be my new symbol for letting go to life and its infinite possibilities.

A thumb's up!

Epilogue

First things first: I honored my end of the Larry deal and watched Curb Your Enthusiasm. Not one, not two, not even ten episodes, but all six seasons. (Though not in one sitting.) I found it brilliant and Larry is terrific. It is easy to see why the show is such a success and people love it. I have yet to watch Seinfeld.

Maybe if Larry gives me another ride I'll check it out.

Since leaving the Island the magic has continued.

One afternoon, while working on the Ted Danson chapter, I got a strong craving for some grapefruit. So I took a break and wandered down to the Whole Foods Market. I picked up my bounty, headed for the checkout counter, turned the corner and ran straight into Ted Danson! For a moment in shock I stood there. Was I hallucinating?

If this were the Vineyard, or even Los Angeles, it would merely be an amazing coincidence. But to see him here in Nashville? No way! Could this be the beginning of *The Ted Phenomenon?* (My next book: Grocery Shopping With Ted Danson)

Ted was standing with his lovely wife, the saintly Mary. In my synchronistic stupor I made a complete fool of myself. (The more things change, the more they stay the same.) I didn't say anything unusually dumb, but I may have come off as just another crazed fan, forcing the poor guy into *The Ted Danson Lean-Back*. Fortunately, after a few tense moments, they recognized me from the Vineyard and we shared a few nice moments.

The other day my friend Dan told me an interesting story. He and his wife decided against cutting down the dead walnut tree and putting a pool in their yard. They went outside, held hands beside the tree, and asked it to come back to life. A few weeks later, they noticed some new growth and within three months the tree had come back fully.

Oh one more thing…I still believe in Miracle(s)!

Acknowledgements

Shortly after I began writing this book, my dear friend Peter Dergee moved in. After watching me hack away on the keyboard for days, he became interested in what I was doing. "Do you mind if I take a look at it? I've done a little editing in my time. Maybe I can help."

So I had the good fortune to have an in-house editor, and a gifted one at that. Peter put in countless hours. The book would be illegible without his contribution. Most importantly, he made what is usually a lonely process lots of fun. If this book were a film, Peter would be its producer.

The Miracle had a huge impact on my rewriting process, instinctively guiding me towards more of this and less of that. Also, I never knew I had such a strict grammarian living under my roof. Sadly, though she repeated the rules that govern grammar countless times they have yet to sink in.

The Great Simmons gave me pages of constructive notes. So did my structure expert, Richard Morton. (Check out his excellent book Stealing Mona Lisa!) Jana Stanfield had some great ideas and suggestions. Michael O. in Atlanta was a great proofreader. These wonderful people also helped raise the book bar: Jill Franks, Marie Bozzetti-Engstrom, Susan Fondren, Dan Casey, and Ann Miracle.

My brother Chris has been a wonderful friend to me for more than forty years. Thanks Bis!

My parents have done an amazing job of putting up with me through the years and have taught me so much about life.

When I think of what they came from I am in awe of whatever love they have been able to manifest.

A special thank you to my many friends who love me so unconditionally: (in no particular order…)

Saint Jack, Neil Warren, The Mighty Cam, Petey, Lucy, Tim, Johnny, Frankie, Threal, Monte, Ma Bevins, Mostopiece, Dennis, Dan Maddox, David, James & Marybeth, Bonnie, Brandon, Danny, Mo, TJ, Bernie & Wendy, Sammy, Billy Block, Tom-Lucas, and lastly my favorite crust-man, Moses.

On the Vineyard: Sam & Emily, Jaime & Eli at the Atlantic, Kevin Butler, David & Rosalee McCullough, Andrew & Angela Brandt, Mrs. Grant, Nicky Weinstock, Anita, Judy & Caroline Sharp.

Oh, and in case I forgot to say it at the time, "Larry thanks for the ride."

Let me know what you think:

mvyhitchhiker@gmail.com

Also...

Please visit my site:

www.hitchhikingwithlarrydavid.com

And...

Become a member...

I would love to stay in touch~

CPSIA information can be obtained at www.ICGtesting.com
264409BV00011B/115/P